Th[...]

MISH-[...]

dictionary

of

MARMITE

an anecdotal A-Z

of

'Tar-in-a-Jar'

By Maggie Hall

Revel Barker
Publishing

First published in 2009 by Revel Barker
Publishing.

Copyright © 2009 Margaret Hall

Cover © Rex Aldred
rex.dred@live.co.uk

Illustrations © Dave Jeffery
www.davejefferyartist.co.uk

ISBN: 978-0-9563686-0-7

Revel Barker Publishing 66 Florence Road
Brighton BN2 6DJ United Kingdom
revelbarker@gmail.com

Author's Note

The mere mention of Marmite provokes passionate – and sharply divided – reaction. Can there be anyone in Britain who has never heard of it? Few can be in the position of never having tasted it.

There is no half-hearted response. As the legendary advertising campaign tells us: you either love it, or hate it. You'd be hard pressed to be in the company of anyone who doesn't have a feeling to express, a memory evoked or an anecdote to tell.

The thought of it, the smell of it, the taste of it, strike physical and mental chords that delve deep back into childhood. But what do most of us know about the black goo? The answer is basically zero.

In fact even most fans would be hard-pressed to answer 'yes', if asked: do you like yeast extract on your toast?

I probably ought to have made it clear, before you forked out your cash – although you may have done that already – that this is not a real 'dictionary'. It is, as the title says, a 'mish-mash'. *The Oxford Dictionary* (now, there's a real one) defines 'mish-mash' as 'a confused collection' or 'hodgepodge'. Others say it means 'curious mixture'. This offering lives up to all three interpretations. One reason for that is that this is an unauthorised version – it comes to you without the blessing of Unilever, owners of Marmite.

The giant food, laundry soap and personal products conglomerate could not give this project its seal of approval – never mind its support, cooperation, or access to the Marmite archives. The barrier was the contracts it had to produce other books on the iconic product whose fame has – quite literally – spread around the world.

But that is my own fault. In 1997 I had the idea to write a book about Marmite but I was thwarted on two fronts. Firstly, interest from the publishing industry was nil. One leading publisher turned down my proposal because there was no sex in it (although there is a bit, ever such a little bit, now). Secondly the then owners of Marmite, CPC, while happy to give me access to records, were not prepared to back the book financially.

So I retreated and returned to journalism, to enjoy generating big headlines, exciting assignments, annoying people who can't stand tabloid reporters. I also withdrew from Marmite and anything and everything allied to it.

But every sight of a jar sent me into a fit of self-pity about not following through on my 'literary project'. Finally, fed up with friends asking 'what happened to your Marmite idea?', I took the plunge. Only to discover that my original idea was all the rage – and I was on the outside, now barely able to get so much as a glimpse into the official Marmite world.

However as a result, and left to my own devices, I uncovered the most amazing, zany, interesting, erudite, amusing, stupid gems of information – all linked by one noun, proper and common: **MARMITE.**

Black magic personified!

MH

MAGGIE HALL has always fallen into the 'love Marmite' category. But until she spied one of the first silver lids many years ago she had no clue as to the huge hold the black goo has on the nation. Her immediate thought was: What's going on here? Now having put this A-Z together she knows that it's a bizarre, serious, zany, wholesome, off-the-wall, carry-on.

As a retired Fleet Street reporter – who started life in Cleckheaton, Yorkshire and now divides her time between Washington DC, Whitby in Yorkshire and travelling – none of what she discovered on this voyage around the world of Marmite should have surprised her. But it did!

Dedicated to: M. L. E.*

* M.L.E? Easy to work out.
Marmite Lovers/Loathers Everywhere!

A

Aaagh: the groan of sheer horror made by someone who can't stand Marmite – particularly when an open jar is wafted under their nose. For some, just the sight of it is enough to set off the verbal grunt of dislike. But for many others, the mere mention of it is enough to provoke sounds of outrage. Even contempt.

Aaaha: the sound of pure pleasure expressed when a Marmite lover spies that familiar brown jar, especially in an unexpected place – like, at a hostel in the middle of the Tikal rain forest in Guatemala. It's hard to describe the feeling of comfort that's swept over many a Brit back-packer at that and similar far-flung sightings.

Accomodata: a British travel web-site. Information on all aspects of 'going somewhere', from hotels and holiday apartments, both at home and abroad, to flights, car rentals, train timetables. So what on earth has any of that got to do with the subject in hand? Nothing really, except that, bizarrely, it hosts a Marmite site...

It tells succinctly the Marmite Story, giving a run-down of its history, nutritional value, and enduring appeal, with some colourful examples of **advertising** over the decades. There's also a section for recipes, submitted by readers of the site. The site also invites those 'with questions about this wonderful product' to e-mail. And they certainly do! Robert Fuller, sales manager at *Accomodata*, which is operated out of Tadworth, Surrey, told me they receive requests for Marmite information from around the world. They've had messages from the Marmite inquisitive in places as remote as Tristan de Cunha, Christmas Island and the Maldives.

The Marmite pages started out as a novelty idea, in the early 'www' days of 1992, in a bid to attract internet browsers to the travel site. Also as a way to attract visitors to Britain, in terms of 'wow, look what they have there'. The statistics show that 65% of people who visit the Marmite Story, go on to look at the travel site. 'Reverse marketing rules,' grinned Robert. So, what's with the incorrect spelling of 'accomodata'? The explanation is easy, though it will sound odd to those who weren't in at the start of the internet. In the beginning technical restrictions meant that a domain name could not exceed 10 letters. So the company dropped an 'm'. Reverse logic scored again. Robert said: 'Our statistics prove that throughout the non-English world 'accommodation' is misspelt 75% of the time. And although we now also own the domain with the name spelt properly, we get more hits on the incorrect spelling.'

***Advertising*:** like the product itself, legendary stuff. From day one, in 1902, Marmite has been advertised in a manner that tracks society. Its changing ways, attitudes and styles have been monitored and captured by the marketing of Marmite.

In the early days, advertisements featured sketches of doctors and nurses, to underline the health-giving qualities of Marmite. Today, the cutting-edge approach has produced award winning campaigns that are the envy of other products, desperate to join Marmite as a kitchen icon. The slogans used by the many agencies involved in promoting Marmite over the past 100-plus years tell the story.

In 1927 the slogan was The Great **Yeast** Food. It was used alongside a sketch of middle-aged man in a bow-tie holding a steaming mug. During World War II it was pushed as a flavourful way of eking out food shortages. Typical of newspaper advertising was the pen and ink drawing of an ageing Harry Potter-type, clutching a large pie straight out of the oven. The main message was: 'MAKES MEAT PIES marvellous!' And then in a clever, for those days, twist on words: 'Insist on MARMITE and you'll get it,' followed by: '...it is the making of all soups, stews... makes the most of war-time rations...' Alongside a picture of Marmite, the size of available jars and prices were listed, starting with 1oz for 6d up to 16oz for 4s/2d.

The ad ended with: 'from all grocers and chemists'. Chemists? As hard as it may be for the younger generation of shoppers to believe, up to around 50 years ago if you wanted olive oil – a product whose benefits were also wisely recognised as basically medicinal – the most likely place to buy it would have been in a pharmacy.

Also during World War II, the advertising agency used an ARP cartoon character, sitting behind a sand-bag wall, clutching a large jar of Marmite, to tell people to 'store some for an emergency'. And, in an extreme move for the day, the ad alongside ARP spelt out: 'All Ready Prepared', instead of what ARP stood for – 'Air Raid Precaution'.

In 1951 the three-M factor came into play. Namely: 'MUCH', 'MORE' and 'MOST'. The varying reasons for its growing popularity were set out, as in: 'MUCH excitement! Marmite on toast for Tea. Always a popular favourite; MORE health-giving, too. Marmite is a natural source of essential B2 vitamins; MOST families go for it in a big way. You never tire of... MARMITE on toast.'

And to illustrate how happy that would make consumers there was a sketch of a smiling, matinee idol-type, holding a piece of toast, smeared in black, with a large bite taken out of it. By now the price for a 1oz jar was up to 8d, a 16oz jar was 5s/9d.

By the mid-50s the ads were urging people to make Marmite a vital part of their sandwiches, particularly during the summer, when the slogan informed: Salad Says are Sandwich Days. Alongside a knife, coated in Marmite, coming out of a jar, there were instructions on how to turn 'crisp lettuce and cool cucumbers' into a sandwich with 'more flavour – and more goodness'. Because, as the advert advised, 'Marmite, as well as being a most delicious savoury spread, is a valuable addition to the diet. It contains health-giving B vitamins'.

In 1960 the good-for-you factor was still being heavily promoted. In the September issue of the *British Medical Journal*, a detailed advertisement pointed out how vital it was for pregnant women, how it could be used in preventive medicine, for those on restricted diets and in the care of the geriatric. By the 1970s the advertising adopted a definite zippy approach with the slogan: The Growing-Up Spread You Never Grow Out Of.

In the 1980s that gave way to the memorable era of: My Mate Marmite. The 1990s was all about the concept of recognising publicly that the product divided the country, households and couples. The Love-Hate campaign is famous in the advertising world. It was a brave move. But it touched a nerve that firmly established, in case there was doubt, that Marmite had achieved cult status.

In the mid-2000s another courageous campaign was launched. It wrenched **Paddington Bear** away from his beloved marmalade, got him eating Marmite – to promote the dubious squeezy jar – and triggered an outpouring of horror. It was roundly condemned. How could the beloved story-book character be used in such a crass, commercial manner? However the controversy did only one thing: it pushed Marmite more firmly into the nation's psyche.

Allergies: sad, but true. Some children, particularly the very young, have an alarming allergy to Marmite, or any yeast extract spread. They break out in hives and sores and breathing can be severely affected. Technically this is called angio-oedema, defined in medical dictionaries as a swelling of the deeper skin tissues, caused by an allergy to food, which triggers the release of histamine in skin-cells.

The Marmite **loveline** – the telephone number 0800-0323656 is on every label – is set up for out-of-hours callers seeking medical help. A recorded message tells them to contact their doctor or call NHS Direct.

The alarm, about this dangerous side-effect of Marmite, was raised some 20 years ago by Dr Nigel Higson. In a letter to the *British Medical Journal*, in January 1989, he wrote: '...allergy to a food containing Marmite seems a common and frightening occurrence, particularly in very young children.' He cited the case of a 15-month-old child who ate Marmite thinly spread on white, buttered, bread. 'Within five minutes mild angio-oedema of the lips and periorbital tissues had occurred,' he reported. 'This caused no difficulty in breathing and subsided within 60 minutes. The link with Marmite was not recognized and some days later the child was again given some on bread. This time a more dramatic reaction occurred, with a greater degree of angio-oedema, such that the child exhibited some difficult in respiration.'

Although the toddler did not require any drug treatment, Dr Higson became so concerned about his allergic reaction to Marmite he made enquiries among his patients with young children. He reported: 'I found that several other young children exhibited similar reactions to Marmite. And, although I know of no major anaphylactic reaction occurring, the angio-oedema is sufficiently severe to cause concern to the parent.'

Dr Higson, who still practices in Hove, Sussex, then issued a warning to health visitors – some of whom he noted advised mothers, trying to wean their babies, to put Marmite on their **nipples** to break the child's breast feeding habit. 'In a susceptible child this action might possibly be fatal,' he concluded.

In February 2009, Marmite being the trigger for nasty outbreaks of hives, spots and bad dreams, was aired on *Mumsnet*, a website where mothers seek advice from others. One, writing about her 33-month old son, said: 'Recently he has taken a shine to Marmite and I'm now wondering if there is a direct correlation between eating it and the spots, the nightmares and feeling unwell? I'm going to stop him eating Marmite to see if it helps, but wondered if anyone else had a similar experience?' There were several responses. One mother confirmed that 'lots' of children get a rash from Marmite and **Bovril**. Another said it was probably the high histamine content in yeast extract, while another recalled how, as a child, Marmite made her feel 'unwell'.

Allison, Sonia: first of the second generation of Marmite **cookery books** – written by celebrity chefs and well known food-writers – was Sonia Allison's. She was one of Britain's most prodigious cookery-book writers and in her 1969 *The Marmite Guide to Better Cooking*, she encouraged the use of it in dozens of imaginative ways, decades before manufacturers got round to adding Marmite to processed products, crisps, crackers, rice-crackers, bread-sticks and cheese. Notable in that category are Sonia's recipe for Marmite Rusks and Marmite Twists.

Also way ahead of its time is her savoury Birthday Cake. This is a large white loaf, with the crusts taken off, cut length-ways into four long slices, then layered with Marmite, cream cheese, canned tuna and 'iced' with mashed hard-boiled eggs, mayo and cream-cheese. Sonia guaranteed it would be a hit because, as she wrote, children's tastes had changed. And she claimed that they gravitated towards the savouries, leaving the jellies, trifles and cakes pretty much untouched. How many parents today, 40 years on, will be wishing that was the case now!

The book, still available from second-hand booksellers on-line, also includes a low-calorie section, complete with the Marmite Diet and some timeless advice about why Marmite is useful to those looking to shed some weight. Sonia wrote: 'Because it is rich in the B vitamins, it acts as a morale booster and prevents that run down, tired and irritable feeling so often experienced by those who are eating less than usual.'

Sonia, who lived in Watford, Hertfordshire, died in 2003, aged 72. Her widower Norman, was delighted to know that Sonia's Marmite book was to be included here. He said: 'Sonia was always ahead of her time. She wrote the first books on micro-wave cooking and bread-machines. She was working as a consultant for Marmite, on the public relations side, and the book just evolved out of that.'

The inscription on the marble headstone of Sonia's grave reads: 'She lives on in her books.' And that is for sure. In 1999 she had huge success with her book on how to produce pickles, preserves and jam, using a microwave. It was republished in June 2009, under the title: *Quick and Easy One Pot of Jam from Your Microwave*.

Alternatives: yes, there are other yeast extracts out there – all with their own loyal followings. Probably more than you would have imagined. Most Marmite lovers know about **Vegemite**, the Australian rival, that is so markedly different, it's hard to think of them being remotely similar. But there are

others. In Britain there is: **Natex** and
Meridian, plus 'own brand' supermarket
versions from Tesco and Asda. In Australia,
Vegemite is challenged by: **Promite**, Mighty
Mate, and a fairly new one, Aussie Mite. New
Zealand has Marmite, but it's nothing to do
with British Marmite. Switzerland has Cenovis,
which is nearly as old as Marmite. South
Africa has Marmite, made under licence for
Unilever. Germany has **Vitam-R**, which sells
well in Britain and the USA – to the surprise of
many – has Vegex. There's quite a collection
of those that failed to stand the test of time –
or rather fell at the mighty feet of Marmite.
Until very recently, in Britain, there was
Toastmate and the organic Crazy Jack. Many
years ago there was **Barmene**, Yeastrel and
Yex. Holland had **Reformite** and Ireland the
sadly lamented **GYE**. More information on
some of them, under appropriate initial or
country.

Ambient: Marmite is many things to many
people. It is a delicious spread, it is a
revolting spread. Take your pick. But to
grocers it is an 'ambient spread'. That is the
category of product the trade put it in. Along
with fish paste, peanut butter, pâtés, honey,
jam, and its stable-companion **Bovril**.

Anaemia: from the outset the manufacturers
knew Marmite was a health promoting product
but it was Dr Lucy Wills who officially pin-
pointed how wonderfully useful its **Folic acid**
ingredient could be in combating anaemia,
particularly during pregnancy. In its October

20, 1934 edition, *Nature* magazine reported that Marmite, while long recognised as a source of the Vitamin B complex, had recently been found of value in treating various types of anaemia.

Art: yes, there is Marmite art. And as the ubiquitous quip goes: 'at last they've found a good use for it!' Marmart, as it's dubbed, was a 2006 publicity campaign organised by Marmite's owners, **Unilever**, in a bid to promote what a good idea it would be to retrieve it from a squeezy bottle. Top illustrator-artist Dermot Flynn was roped in.

He produced 10 pieces of toast, all adorned with a squeezy likeness of a group of you-either-love-'em-or-hate-'em personalities. Those featured were music mogul Simon

Cowell; former prime minister Margaret Thatcher; WAG and occasional singer Victoria 'Posh' Beckham; singers Charlotte Church and James Blunt; Conservative leader David Cameron; chef Gordon Ramsay; actor Jude Law; bad-boy rocker Pete Doherty, and Big Brother contestant Nikki Grahame.

Frankly it was difficult to identify some of them. But thanks to the sway that anything Marmite has on many, the 'art' was hung in the prestigious Air Gallery in London's Dover Street. And no, the squeezy impregnated toast collection was not eaten afterwards. It was put up for auction, on e-Bay and bought for the lofty sum of £920 by Wayne **Withers** – as a Christmas present for his wife Lisa.

ART-2: The **Marmite Prize**! This is the wonderful, off-the-wall - literally sometimes - art contest that's held every two years.

B

Baldness: a myth that refuses to die is that Marmite can cure or reverse hair-loss. The theory, fuelled by the rich amounts of B-vitamins in Marmite, was first uncovered in 1995 by researcher Jonathan Langley. During a study of urban myths and legends he discovered that men – especially Northerners – were given to smearing Marmite on their shiny-pates.

In a letter to *Marketing Week* magazine, he revealed: 'Appreciable, and sometimes spectacular, regrowth is said to result when Marmite is liberally and regularly applied to balding heads and left overnight.' He added: 'Converts are easily recognised by their curiously coloured, ebony hair and a pervasive odour.' But there was no proof it worked. 'As with all classic urban myths, there is naturally not a hair of corroborative evidence to substantiate this highly dubious story,' he wrote.

Writer Kevin Baldwin reminded us of this bizarre trend in his 2005 book *Bald!* Kevin – whose last name is perfect for somebody writing about hair-loss – recalled the woman from Lancashire who contacted *Take a Break* to reveal that her shiny-headed husband had tried the Marmite-treatment before going to bed one night. She told the magazine that the outcome was that the Marmite set solid and stuck his head to the pillow. And he was stuck with no improvement in hair-growth – as well as having to confess what a silly idea it was. But then *his* surname was Burke...

"I think I'm supposed to leave it on for a while, not have someone lick it off..."

Banned: Marmite, in TV **advertising** during children's programming has been banned since 2007. Along, it must be pointed out, with a huge slew of other everyday British pantry products. This all to do with the HFSS policy (ie high in fat, salt and sugar). Although **Unilever** fought the ban – there's more salt in the bread on which it's spread than Marmite itself, is a basic salvo of the company – it was reinforced in December 2008.

Banned-2: Since September 2008, Marmite has been off the 'breakfast club' menu for 51 schools under the authority of Ceredigion County Council, which covers the Aberystwyth area. Again, it's the high salt content that's got it into trouble. As a spokeswoman for the education department explained to me: 'It's too salty. And because of that it is not on our approved list.' However the children are free to take their own Marmite sandwiches into school for breakfast or lunch.

Banned-3: before the total **advertising** ban during children's programming, one famous Marmite commercial got the heave-ho by the Advertising Standards' Authority. In 2004 it banned the infamous 'blob' ad, which used a clip from the legendary Steve McQueen sci-fi horror movie of 1958, *The Blob*.

In the ad the 'blob' was depicted as a huge mountain of Marmite rolling down the street. People start running from it, but then some turn back and dive into it! Half a dozen parents complained that after viewing the ad their children refused to watch television, or had nightmares. While the Broadcasting Advertising Clearance Centre decreed that the ad displayed 'very mild horror that was clearly comical,' the ASA begged to differ – and ruled that it raised enough concern to be restricted to being shown in the evening only. No mention was ever made of the number of adults who then went on to suffer nightmares.

Barmene: no longer around, but a one-time rival to Marmite. The name was an extension of the noun *barm*, which is defined as the froth on any fermenting product – including, of course, **yeast**. The label carried a picture of a monk. There must have been a reason for that... but not one that I've been able to uncover.

Beginnings: once up a time, centuries ago, the brewers of Europe used to look in horror at the yeast-sludge left behind by the process. It was tough to dispose of. While some would be smuggled out of the brewery by hard-up workers with families to feed, and bucketfuls would be thrown to the pigs to gobble up, most was tossed out. Which is why some stretches of the famous rivers of Europe and Britain presumably ran a dark, murky brown. (I have no evidence for that last bit – but where else would they have disposed of it?)

Then along came the Dutch scientist Anton van Leeuwenhoek. He's famed for two things: inventing the microscope and almost, but not quite, discovering Marmite. It was in 1680 that Leeuwenhoek decided enough was enough. Surely there was something worthy buried deep in the mounds of brewery waste that was just going well, to waste. He started poking around in some of it using, of course, the new-fangled device he'd just invented. Being a citizen of Amsterdam he had plenty of breweries to plunder. Through his infant microscope he was astonished to see the **yeast** mess was made up of minuscule, spherical-shaped cells. But his excitement over having built a microscope must have superseded any enthusiasm he had of doing more research into the yeast-cells. (Apart from that, there is no clue to why he didn't pursue the yeast lead!)

Almost two hundred years passed, during which time the world got plenty of microscopes but no hint of Marmite, before those perfect, beautiful, just waiting to be used, cells got looked at again. This time it was the two greatest scientific minds of the day that came together to finish what the Dutch scientist had started. Louis Pasteur took time off from combating germs, anthrax and rabies, and making milk safe to drink, to apply his micro-biology talents to brewer's sludge. His research showed that one grain of yeast contained millions of cells, which in turn measured barely 1/3000th of an inch. He determined that each cell was a living plant, possessing a well defined and complex structure. Something could, and should, be done with this mess.

Enter the brilliant German chemist, Baron Justus von Liebig, whose expertise was starting with a substance and extracting something desperately useful. He was already famous for having discovered nitrogen and its use as a fertilizer, and for extracting liquid from meat, resulting in his inventing Oxo and founding the Fray Bentos company. Like Pasteur, doing something with the yeast mess was a challenge he accepted with enormous vitality. He knew, thanks to his pal Pasteur, that it had the potential to take it far away from its 'yukky' status. Something worthy could and would be salvaged from the hideous residue. After all it was yeast. And both men knew its properties bode well for the future of toast around the world. After all, they'd already proved that each cell contained 50%, of high-nutritional protein. But how to get it into palatable form?

After much trial and error, von Liebig came up with a process that turned the waste into a substance that not only looked vaguely edible, but smelled and tasted acceptable. The key to the mystery was unlocked when he subjected the yeast to autolysis. That is defined in the *Concise Oxford Dictionary*, as 'destruction of cells of the body by the action of its own serum'. In other words a process of self-digestion.

In 1873, long before he saw his dream of a meatless extract come into commercial being, von Liebig died. Finally a patent on the technique was awarded. But it kept being sold on, as group after group tried to market the result. Success was not only poor, it didn't exist. The hard scientific work had been done, and while it was thought possible to convert the brewery waste into a tasty product, it was far from simple. Pasteur died in 1895, so also failed to live to see his discovery end up in pantries around the world.

It wasn't until 1902 the Brits – who had as much sludge on their beery hands as anyone

– entered the picture. In the heart of the City of London, in a suite of offices in an elegant Georgian house called Mincing Lane House, a group of business men plotted how to pry the patent away from the Continent. While popular belief always talks about a British consortium being responsible for bringing the formula to Britain, it was in fact led by a German; retired sugar merchant Frederick Wissler headed the group. Any reference to Herr Wissler in the history of Marmite is virtually lost. But whatever his connection, it probably came via the aforementioned von Liebig. Anyway, eventually the Brits met the Continental owners and long negotiations were entered into. Finally they were concluded on June 13, and the Marmite Food Extract Company Limited, was formed. And the rest, as they say, is a long, tasty, disgusting, super, hideous, love-hate affair with virtually every man, woman and child in Britain. Make that the world. Heck, make it the Universe!

Boils: Is it really necessary to bring up such a horrid condition in a book about food? Yes, because – being the wonder product of the world – Marmite has inevitably been highly recommended for the treatment of boils. A young woman, identified only as Miss LC, wrote to the now long gone *Healthy Life Magazine* pleading for help in finding relief from boils. 'I have been suffering from a recurrence of boils on different parts of my body for the last six months,' she wrote. 'I have consulted a doctor who can find no reason for their appearance but suggested I should try a mixed diet, to include some animal food, rather than adhere to vegetarianism as I have done for some two years past.'

The answer revealed how drugs or medicines were of little use, because they failed to get to the root of the trouble. But fresh or dried brewer's **yeast** was – even if unpleasant to take – a highly effective remedy. It went on to say how it contained nuclein and nucleinic acid, which were chemically identical to the same substances found in human cells, and were a powerful antiseptic. 'It is for this reason that yeast extracts, such as Marmite, often have a beneficial effect in disorders accompanied by the formation of pus matter.'

The magazine detailed a diet that Miss L C should follow. It allowed her to stick to a vegetarian diet, and heavily featured Marmite, taken as a drink. Her day was to start with a mug of Marmite, another one mid-afternoon and finally, as a nightcap. That advice was dished-up in the July-December 1913 issue. But there is no reason why it wouldn't work just as well today!

Books: Marmite makes an appearance in thousands of them. A wonderful way of wasting a huge amount of time is to enter 'marmite' into the Amazon website. The UK site brings up more than three thousand books in which the word appears, but the American site has double that number. Both sites have a handy 'look inside this book' search tool that pulls up the page where the inserted word appears. It will take you days to work through all the entries. I got as far as entry number 992, on page 84, when the computer went wonky and bounced me off the internet. But by then I'd got the picture. Hundreds of novels – with characters mundanely munching on breakfast toast covered with the stuff, to its being used in fun sex games and even as a threat, such as: if you don't do as I say you will be force-fed this black-goo that you totally despise. Plus of course publications with references to: the French cooking pot of the same name; petit Marmite, the French soup; the name of restaurants. It's also mentioned in countless travel books, as well as medical guidance tomes, particularly in relation to **anaemia** in pregnancy; **depression**; **gout**; eating disorders and **migraine**.

Bovril: it will come as a surprise to some fans to learn that Marmite and Bovril are owned by the same company. And to many that do know that **Unilever** is in charge of both, it will probably come as a shock to know that the two great British black-goo spreads have been joined through ownership since 1924. Bovril pre-dates Marmite by 16 years. It was invented by Scot, John Lawson Johnston. His son, George Lawson Johnston, carried on the business and was created a hereditary peer in 1929. It was his son, Ian St John Lawson Johnston – the second Baron Luke – who acquired Marmite. His business sense told him that it was not a take-over that should be shouted from the roof-tops. Even then, tastes and opinion, dictated a wide divide between the two products with consumers shunning one in favour of the other. So, while close inspection of the label would reveal that Marmite was made by Bovril Ltd., the togetherness was not advertised or talked about for fear users would think the actual products were merged in the jar. That policy became even more important when the original Bovril factory in Old Street, Shoreditch, in the City of London, was closed and the manufacture of the beefy-product was moved to **Burton-on-Trent**, to be made alongside Marmite. In 1970, the stable-mates succumbed to a hostile takeover by corporate-raider James Goldsmith's, Cavenham Foods. That triggered other deals over the years that saw the iconic twin products being sold on several times before finding sanctuary with Unilever in 2000.

Bread: it's not just crack-pots who do things with Marmite other than put it on their toast. Pru Leith, one of the original celebrity chefs, urges the 'love it' brigade to make their favourite breakfast, or sandwich, a 'double-dipper'. In 2004, Pru – who is due to end a three year stint as chair of the School Food Trust in January 2010 – published her recipe for Marmite bread in the *Daily Mail*. It's a no-brainer but like so many other things in life, it often takes someone else to point out the obvious. Variations on the recipe are found all over the place now. Basically all you do is one of two things: either mix some Marmite into the milk, or oil, your recipe calls for; or twirl some through the finished dough – so it looks 'rippled'.

Bulimia: two of the world's leading experts in eating-disorders recommend Marmite as a friend to those struggling with the disease. In books considered 'Bibles' they both include Marmite in diets to aid recovery. In *Overcoming Bulimia and Binge Eating* – first published in 1993 and updated in 2007 – Dr Peter Cooper, professor of psychology at Reading University, has a How-to-Stop-Dieting diet. Lunch, on the second day, is: a Marmite (or fish paste) sandwich, an apple, a slice of fruit cake and fruit juice. Professor Bryan Lask, of St George's Hospital, London, has a similar diet in *Anorexia Nervosa and Related Eating Disorders in Childhood and Adolescence*, published in 2000. His weight-gaining diet for a teenage girl, lists an afternoon snack as: toast, butter and Marmite.

Burton-on-Trent: the ancestral home of Marmite. Manufacture of it began in the Staffordshire town in 1902 in a disused malt house on Cross Street. As spent brewer's **yeast** is the base of Marmite, Burton – the traditional home of British beer – was the obvious choice for Marmite to set up shop. In those days Burton boasted 32 breweries, with the legendary Bass as the biggest of the lot.

Now there are only three breweries. Originally all the waste yeast came from Bass. Some of it still does, but Bass is now just one of the many beers owned by the Canadian-American consortium of Moulson-Coors. The other brewery in town, that supplies Marmite today, is Wolverhampton and Dudley Breweries that brews Marston's. The third, the Bridge Brewery, is a 'micro' operation with its own pub. Its 'sludge', which presumably is as wonderful as its range of 'designer' ales, would make a terrific Marmite-starter. But it does not produce enough to make it worthwhile for Unilever to cart it the couple of miles to the Marmite factory.

In 1953 Marmite moved into bigger premises on what was then Wellington Street. By 1967 a new purpose-built complex, on the industrial site on what had become Wellington Road, became the joint Marmite-**Bovril** factory. In those days both names appeared on the factory premises. Today the Marmite jar logo is displayed on a somewhat tatty old water-tower. There is no mention of Bovril: probably all part of the policy to try and keep public attention away from the fact they share factory premises. Also, as this book went to press, a For Sale sign of 'site and premises' went up, at the entrance... Enquiries revealed that six freehold acres were up for grabs. It's hard to believe that Unilever would do what the For Sale hints at: ie transfer the manufacture of Marmite elsewhere. It was probably more to do with Unilever unloading the part of the factory that was devoted to the production of Pot Noodles, which was transferred to Norwich in 2008.

Considering that Marmite is a national treasure, it's amazing the scant attention it gets in Burton. Visitors could come and go and never realise they're spending time in the home-town of one of Britain's most famous products. The only mention is, in passing, on a poster located around town, naming the people and things that have put Burton on the map. Marmite does not get its own section, but is incorporated into one devoted to William Bass, founder of the Bass Brewery. After saying how he arrived in Burton from London in 1777, the item continues: 'One of the things Burton-on-Trent is famous for is the production of the I love it or hate it MARMITE'.

And I had been expecting, when I got off the train, I'd be greeted with a sign that proclaimed: 'Welcome to Burton - Home of Marmite'. Instead the station sign says: 'A Gateway to the National Forest'. And after that, lots of signs pointing the way to the Coors' Visitor Centre, Marston's Brewery, plus the original site of Bass being pinpointed with a steel name-plate in the pavement.

Another shock was how few people knew where the factory was. Responses ranged from: 'I've no idea,' to 'it's around here somewhere.' Even the driver of the bus I took to go to the factory, hadn't a clue. 'I can't tell you which is the nearest stop because I don't know where it is,' she said. In the end I got off at the right stop, but only because I spotted, in the distance, the Marmite jar on the water-tower. I thought I would be treading a popular path – to pay homage to the factory where the spread I've loved for ever is made. But no. As the guard at the security gate told me: 'No, love – you're the first I've known to be interested in that way.' So before I asked whether there were tours of the factory, I knew the answer! But it's not surprising people aren't banging on the doors of the factory to be allowed a peep inside: no mention is made of Burton-on-Trent even on the label. There hasn't been since Unilever took it over.

Would-be prime minister David Cameron has done his small bit to keep the image of Marmite-in-Burton alive. In June 2009 he campaigned in the town. His opening remark had nothing to do with politics but were about enjoying the good things in life. 'It's great to be here in the home of Marmite and beer,' he enthused.

C

Cakes: when Letitia, the zany parishioner in the TV comedy *Vicar of Dibley*, made a Marmite cake for Frank's birthday, viewers roared.

To many it's not a laughing matter but one

where that numero uno favourite food is merged with the unlikely!

The South Africans, who are as crazy about Marmite as the Brits, are proud of what they claim is their invention – Cheese and Marmite cake. The cake itself is a conventional Victorian sponge. It's the 'icing' that gives it that big-M taste. Melt equal amounts of butter with Marmite, spread over the top of the cake, then sprinkle with grated Cheddar cheese. Since the recipe was printed in South Africa's *You* magazine in 1987 it's gone round the Marmite world.

But the cake student Sophia Simpson of Peckham, South London, made in 2008 for her brother Rob's 26th birthday, was something else... She rashly promised she would merge his top three favourite foods, forgetting that Marmite was in that trio! The others were melon and gooseberries. But, boy, did it work out well! Sophie made, like the South African version, a classic Victoria sponge, but added a lot more Marmite. She cut it in half, filling it with a layer of Marmite and sliced melon and gooseberries. She topped it with vanilla icing, decorated with melon pieces and whole gooseberries, then drizzled with Marmite. Sophie, so taken with pulling-off a Marmite impossible, blogged about it on: *www.flickr* (the site to share photos and the stories around them).

She wrote: 'I was seriously – seriously – worried about this. A Marmite cake? Surely not. But in fact it was goooooood! It produced a few worried looks when it was produced but those brave enough to try it discovered it was sweet with a good tang to it. The saltiness somehow enhanced the flavour just enough. I thought it was delicious. If it had been something other than a Victoria sponge I don't think it would have worked. But it was the almost bland sweetness of the cake and the mix of the fruit and the slightly biting saltiness that made it popular. The melon added a sweet lightness and the gooseberries bridged the gap. They were just on the right side of tartness to mingle well. I would recommend this cake – but only if you're truly brave of heart!' Sophie told me she was studying creative writing; she's certainly got the 'creative' bit off pat... when it comes to cake-making.

Caspa: is one of Britain's foremost exponents of the musical movement known as 'dubstep'. It grew out of the garage scene of the early 2000s, and is highly syncopated, with an emphasis on a big bass sound. Londoner Caspa, whose real name is Gary McCann, released his first album *Everybody's Talking* in early 2009. A major track was called *Marmite* which, according to electronic dance music critic Simon Reynolds, had more to do with the slang use of Marmite (see **Rhyming slang**) than Caspa's appreciation of the spread.

Cats: never leave an unopened jar around cats. They love it. And they will lap it up, usually after sending the jar crashing to the floor! It's also a sure-fire way of getting pills down them. Just break up the medication and mash it into a dollop of Marmite.

8 out of 10 cats purr... fer...

Champagne: was added to Marmite to mark Valentine's Day, 2008. The amount of champagne added was so minuscule a lot of folk wondered why they'd bothered! Less than a drop of Bubbly was added to the black stuff. Officially it made up 0.3% of a 250gram jar. And all it did was make the Marmite slightly more runny. Of course if a decent swig had been added then the Marmite would have been sloshing around! As it was it was a fun and clever stroke of marketing. The Marmite-punters were pulled in with the I Love You, heart-shaped front label, and the cute Eros firing off the cork of a Champagne bottle. On the back it said To My Marmite Lover, with a space for the giver to write his or her name. And 18 months later an amazing number of the 600,000 jars of 'fizzy-mite' were selling on e-Bay.

Charles (Prince): On very good authority we know that HRH is a huge fan of Marmite: and in a very precise, sandwich, way. When Herve Marchand, the French-born chef, left the kitchen at Chatsworth House – after the death of Andrew Cavendish, the 11th Duke of Devonshire – he revealed all. In an interview with the *Daily Mail* in 2005, he opened up about the type of picnic sandwich HRH, a regular visitor to the Peak District estate, insists on when out riding or shooting. M. Marchand called the assembly of it one of the Prince's 'more bizarre' habits.

He revealed: 'Apparently the Prince likes his sandwiches just so.' The 'just so' meant building the sandwich in the order in which he was instructed by HRH's personal chef at Highgrove. It involved a split home-made **organic** bap, exactly eight centimetres across. One half was covered in mayonnaise, followed by pesto, shredded mixed green leaves, a cold over-easy fried egg, two thin slices of Gruyere, then topped with the other half, buttered with 'a small layer' of Marmite.

Cheese: keep your eyes open for the cheese stalls at farmers' markets, country fairs and agricultural shows. With a bit of luck you might spy a round of Marmite-Cheese. OK, so

Unilever, in conjunction with Ilchester Cheese, of Somerset, now produces an official supermarket Marmite cheese. Fans rave about it. But small cheese-makers have been mixing yeast extract into Cheddar for around 10 years. It is mouth-wateringly gorgeous – because it has more yeast extract than the one produced under the Marmite label. The 'unofficial' version is easily spotted because of its mottled, orange-brown gleam. It is not, of course, something that everyone is going to stick on their cracker and gobble up. Like any other product that is infused with Marmite, it's a sure fire way of separating the lovers from the loathers. It's the way that when offered or suggested, not a word is said. The reply comes embedded in that crunched-up, disdainful stare that says: what is wrong with you?

Chocolate: yes of course! Marmite and chocolate are wonderful together. Say some. (see **Young, Paul A**).

Cocktails: forget the Worcester sauce; mix a teaspoon or so of Marmite into vodka and tomato juice for the best Bloody Mary you might ever enjoy. A classic Margarita can also benefit from a Marmite twist. Instead of dipping the glass into a bowl of salt, before adding the tequila, triple-sec and fresh lime juice, give it a quick Marmite dunk. After all, salt is salt.

Cookery books: using Marmite in cooking was well established long before 2003, when Paul Hartley's much heralded *Marmite*

38

Cookbook hit the shelves. The first Marmite cookery books (see under **First**) date back to the earliest of its days, and were published, and issued free, by its original owners, the Marmite Food Extract Company Limited. Then in 1969, when Marmite was owned by **Bovril** Group Marketing Ltd, **Sonia Allison**, one of Britain's most productive cookery book writers, put it under the culinary spotlight in *The Marmite Guide to Better Cooking.* In 1981, while still under the stewardship of Bovril, came the *Best of British Cooking*, by another well established cookery writer, **Mary Norwak**. The next book was Rosemary Moon's *My Mate Marmite In the Kitchen* published in 1992, under the auspices of its then owners CPC Ltd. All three books can still be found in second-hand books shops, on amazon.co.uk or e-Bay.

Cosmetics: got problem skin? Plagued with acne, eczema, rosacea, psoriasis? Yes... another nice topic! But yeast extract could hold the secret to finding a cure. We're not suggesting sufferers slather it straight from the Marmite jar, but some of the highest rated facial creams on the market, aimed at bringing relief to irritated skin, are loaded with yeast extract.

A leader in this field is the French skin care company, Biologique Recherche. It claims its Masque Vivant detoxifies and purifies the skin, relieving redness and balancing oils, bringing aid to those with acne and seborrheic skin. Its Creme Dermopurifiante is said to have antibacterial properties that allow it to clear up the redness and irritation associated with the afore-mentioned conditions and provide an even tone to the skin. Both products list 'yeast extract' – which has a stimulating effect on cell metabolism – first in the list of active ingredients. From the company's Paris headquarters, spokeswoman Ingrid Plater told me: 'We use brewer's yeast extract because of its purifying qualities, which have been known since time immemorial.'

Another company using yeast extract in its facial creams is Dainty. 'We've used it for 20 years,' manager Patricia Poon, told me, from the company's Hong Kong headquarters. She also sent a rundown of why it is so useful in facial creams for problem skins. The statement said: 'Yeast extract is composed of many valuable substances like proteins, peptides and amino acids, storage compounds, enzymes and polysaccharides, as well as B-vitamins. The yeast extract used here has a stimulating and activating effect on cell metabolism. The cell's vitality is improved. Yeast extract also promotes collagen synthesis, acts as an anti-inflammatory and soothes, moisturizes and revitalises.'

Neither Biologique Recherche or Dainty are available in Britain. The former is on sale through-out mainland Europe and the USA. The latter is big in Australia, the USA and the far East. But they can be obtained mail-order, via their respective websites.

Cream Cheese: there is nothing new about

mixing Marmite with cream cheese. For many it is the number one way of eating it. But in South Africa – where Marmite is made under licence for **Unilever** and is exactly the same as in Britain – they don't have to bother putting the two together. It comes already mixed. And it's not just a fad; it's been on the market for many years. The combo has never been offered to British consumers. But **Vegemite** has caught-on to what a good idea it is and started producing its own take on the two together. True to the traditional Vegemite way it asked the public to come up with a name for the 'new' product. The first jars to hit the market, mid-2009, went on sale with a 'Name Me' label.

Cricket: this is not about Marmite sandwiches in the club-house at the tea break. It's about 'the Ashes' and the most charismatic umpire ever to wind six jumpers round his waist. To mark the 2009 Ashes series and 'welcome' the **Vegemite** loving Aussies to England, a limited edition jar of Marmite was produced. It was covered to resemble a shiny red cricket ball. In gold, on the back was written: Cricket is like Marmite – entirely eccentric, wholly British and something the rest of the world will never truly understand'. (Unless, of course, you come from Australia, New Zealand, South Africa, India, Pakistan or the Caribbean. But let's not digress....) It was signed: 'Dickie Bird', the legendary former Yorkshire and Leicestershire player and international umpire.

Although Dickie put his name to the prose he didn't know what it said until I told him. 'I just left it to them,' he said. 'I knew they wouldn't let me down.' He was surprised to get a call about the special edition. A month after it hit the supermarkets he still didn't know it had gone on sale. 'I'd better get one – it'll be a nice souvenir.'

The betting is that it will sit in his collection of cricket memorabilia, unopened. So he's not a fan? Let's put it this way: he never felt compelled to pack a jar when he went on his lengthy cricket trips. 'I never have it,' he admitted. Realising such a confession might not go down too well with **Unilever**, he added: 'Well... now and then on a Rivita.'

Unilever also co-opted Marston's onto the cricket-jar team. It provided a little bit of the left-over **yeast** – from the brewing process of its Pedigree bitter – for the special-edition. But it didn't amount to much: only 10% of the total yeast extract used. It's not like it had to be transported a long way; Marston's is brewed in **Burton-on-Trent**, just down the road from the Marmite factory.

Half-a-million cricket-ball jars were produced, for sale in all the usual places. Though even before you could shout 'Owzat', most of them seemed to be on e-Bay!

Crisps: who would ever imagine that 'war' could break out over a bag of crisps? But one is raging over the new Marmite-flavoured variety. Since 2002 Marmite crisps have been part of a Marmite lover's life. Fans had no problem with them as they munched them down by the handful. But in 2009 things changed. Walker's – Britain's number one crisp maker – stopped making them and Unilever (owner of Marmite) started producing them under its own label. But the switch-over was not exactly seamless. In typical Marmite style, the crisp-camp was divided: some loved the new ones, others hated them. The official Marmite Forum on www.Marmite.co.uk was swamped with comments. 'A thousand times better than Walker's,' read one. 'What a let down,' said another. 'Not a patch on Walker's.' The bloggers also got into the taste-test. 'I think they are heaven,' wrote one. 'They're not as nice,' said another. The taste change was put down to a heftier dose of infused Marmite – and the addition of garlic powder.

Cubes: it seems hard to understand but Marmite stock cubes have never taken off. Well, they have, but they've never been allowed to survive. They were first introduced in 1930. Sold in distinctive green and gold tins they were a hit but before long the bosses decided to concentrate on the spread and they were taken off the market, only to be relaunched in 1995. But when **Unilever** took over Marmite the cube days were numbered. It's never been said but it has to be assumed that the massive challenge from Oxo was the main reason for the double-demise of Marmite cubes. In the summer of 2009 four cubes were offered for sale on e-Bay!

Cyanocobalamin: What the deuce is that? Go back a few years and you might remember – that's if you read the label closely: it was an ingredient and was the last item listed. It's the synthetic form of vitamin B-12. These days the Marmite label makes no mention of cyanocobalamin. It just states B-12. Unlike the label on **Meridian** – one of the Marmite alternatives – which still uses the name.

The most chemically complex of the B vitamins, it is another of those vital ingredients that if we didn't get enough of we'd be in the most dreadful, physical and mental, shape. A deficiency is an underlying cause of pernicious anaemia, and potentially severe and irreversible damage to the heart and brain. B-12 is found naturally in meat, chicken, liver, shellfish, milk and eggs, but not yeast extract. So – whether it's referred to as cyanocobalamin or B-12 – it is added. The Meridian version of yeast extract contains significantly more than Marmite, while Vegemite contains none. Maybe that's why it doesn't taste the same!

D

Dab: there are those who swear a dab of Marmite does wonders for all manner of ailments. Not a dab taken – but put on. It's been cited as a cure for cold sores and mouth ulcers. There are whacko stories about mothers coating the chest of a bronchial child with it, so they can breathe in the 'goodness'. Personally I've always felt that, in an emergency, Marmite applied topically to a scratch or any open wound would work as a cure. After all...salt!

Decor: there is no end to the uses an empty Marmite jar can be put to. Actually – besides using it as a pen/pencil desk tidy or as a seedling pot for **plants** – that's a total exaggeration. But you could always be totally imaginative and build a wall! That's exactly what is happening at the Gibela Backpackers Lodge, in Durban, South Africa. Why? Elmar Neethling, who runs the award-winning hostel, makes no bones about it. 'It's for decor,' he laughed, when I asked him about it.

The empty jars will be stuck onto a new wall that will separate the lodge's pool area from the lavatory block. The jars will cover the wall, and the exposed bits – between the neck and the roundness of the jars – will be painted Marmite orange-red. To ensure the huge advert wall for Marmite is seen to best effect at night, fairy lights will be wound in and around the 'decor' touches. Elmar expects the project to take up to four years to complete. He's worked out that time-line because he reckons it typically takes an average family two to three months to finish a jar. But as there is nothing 'average' about Marmite, he might well be surprised how quickly that wall is built! Within three weeks of coming up with the idea, in mid-2009, he had a pile of 30 jars. And he was expecting them to flood in, from around the world, when a plea was posted on the *Back in Africa* website travel forum.

It said: 'Gibela Lodge urgently needs your help! They are trying to cover/build a wall entirely from empty Marmite jars. If you would like to participate in the construction, please post your empty jars to: Gibela, c/o Avondale Road Post Office, Durban, 4101, South Africa.'

In Zulu, 'gibela' translates as 'hop on'. The lodge is hoping tons of Marmite lovers, with tons of empty jars, will hop onto this fun project. And, yes – if you want to spend money on the postage – send your empty ones. They will fit into the wall plan, as the Marmite in South Africa, is made under licence for **Unilever**, and comes in exact look-alike, jars.

Definition: a daft one; but a true story. An American friend who'd never hard of Marmite asked: 'Marmite? What's that? A baby marmot?' And if you don't get it, because you only know Marmot as a make of outdoor gear, a marmot is a rodent mainly found in North America and Eurasia.

Depression: if you're taking an MAO (menoamine oxidase) inhibitor drug, prescribed for depression or Parkinson's Disease, Marmite should be on your banned list. The drug can interact badly with tyramine, a chemical naturally found in Marmite. The result can be appalling headaches, palpitations, nausea, vomiting and dangerously high blood pressure.

Diana (Princess of Wales): Her childhood, though privileged - and sad, because of her mother's desertion - was similar to that of many other British youngsters when it came to tea-time. That part of the day she shared with her brother Charles, after their older sisters, Sarah and Jane, had gone to boarding school. In her 1999 biography, *Diana: In Search of Herself*, writer Sally Bedell Smith revealed, while talking about Diana's father, Earl Spencer: 'Each day, Johnnie made an effort to have tea with his two younger children, a ritual he savoured. "He was never happier than when he was eating Marmite sandwiches and drinking glasses of milk in the nursery," said a neighbour.'

Dictionary: in 1930, Marmite – with a capital 'M' - made its debut in the *Oxford English Dictionary*. The definition read, as it does today: noun, trademark, a dark savoury spread made from yeast extract and vegetable extract.

Diet: when writer and broadcaster Flic Everett faced-up to shedding a few pounds she made Marmite central to her diet. She shunned bread and replaced it with Marmite Rice Cakes. After dropping from size 12 to a size 8 in five months, Flic burst into print about her achievement. In May 2009, she recounted her experience in the *Daily Mail* about getting into shape aided by Marmite. And in praise of her bread substitute she revealed how she felt about the Marmite infused rice cakes – 'a strange yet satisfying addiction'.

Flic, who also runs one of Britain's best vintage clothing boutiques, Rags to Bitches, in Manchester, told me: 'I found replacing bread with the rice-cakes very effective, as I could eat more food for less calories. But plain rice-cakes taste like ceiling tiles – so having ones that actually tasted of something was a huge help. I would eat two or three rice-cakes for breakfast, with hummus or cheese. Then I'd have one as a snack, and probably, if I was hungry, a couple later at night.' Flic, who has always loved Marmite, added: 'I think it's very underrated as a dieting aid. Being on a diet is incredibly boring, so anything low-calorie that genuinely tastes of something is a huge bonus.'

But did her diet put her off Marmite Rice Cakes for ever? 'No, I still love them!'

Dissertation: now we've heard it all! Ali Fearon graduated from Lancaster University with a BA 2:1 degree in history. She wrote her dissertation on Marmite. And, as she admitted to me: 'I got away with it!' Ali's original plan was to secure her degree with a paper on medieval times. She started work on it, but was not excited with the 'rather safe subject' she'd chosen. She kept being drawn back to the idea she'd had at the start of her university life: tracing national identity through a product, or an icon.

This thought was sparked by her childhood in which her family moved from Wiltshire to Ireland, to Belgium and finally the Lake District. As Ali explains: 'I think this is what made me really interested in perceptions of identity and nationality – and items and icons with that kind of association.' Marmite fitted the bill perfectly. One of her tutors told her to 'go for it'. The department could only say no. But it didn't. And the head told Ali that while he'd been looking forward to her medieval paper, he was 'intrigued' how her Marmite thesis would turn out.

It turned out well... very well. 'Key to my

dissertation was whether Marmite could be considered to reflect British identity,' Ali said. 'The conclusion was that it can.' And she reached this conclusion after focusing on Marmite's legendary and ever-changing **advertising**, scouring the internet and interviewing a huge number of fellow students.

Ali, who works as a development project manager for an East Sussex housing association, feared her academic approach to Marmite might put her off ever eating it again. It didn't. 'I absolutely love it and still can't get enough,' she said. And she joked: 'It's certainly a rather sad and large part of my life. Friends and colleagues always poke fun. But they encourage it, leaving things on my desk. Most recently that has been Marmite cashews, home-made Marmite muffins and anything Marmitey they see, like t-shirts and cycling jerseys.'

Dualit: the manufacturers of kitchen appliances have made toasters for more than 60 years. For the Christmas 2005 trade, it went into partnership with Marmite. They didn't come up with a device that etched a Marmite jar onto a slice of bread as it was being toasted: they just slapped Marmite, in the recognisable font, on the sides of a two-slicer, added a bit of red and yellow detail and a best-seller was created. The £134 price tag did not deter sales – and still doesn't. The 'Marmite toaster' is here to stay...

Dysentery: the consumption of Marmite is

well recorded as being an aid to those stricken by dysentery. This is all to do with those massive doses of Vitamin-B it contains. Celebrity/socialite/heiress Jemina Khan found out about its worth the hard way. While married to cricketer-turned politician Imran Khan, she lived in his home country, Pakistan, for nine years. In October 2006, as an ambassador for UNICEF, she returned to see how funds, donated to help those whose lives were devastated by the earthquake a year earlier, were being spent. On the trip she told the London *Evening Standard* that while she lived in Pakistan she suffered badly from regular bouts of amoebic dysentery. As a result for her trip back, she packed Marmite – which her late father, Jimmy Goldsmith, owned via his Cavenham Foods company, in the early to mid-70s – in case she needed to rely on its restorative virtues.

E

Earthenware: the first Marmite, in 1902, was sold in white earthenware jars. It wasn't until 1928 that the dark brown glass jar – basically the same as it is today – took over.

East Staffordshire: the local authority for Burton-on-Trent, which is home to the Marmite factory and the borough council's town hall. It recognises the fame of its historic home-town product in a fun way. They've set up a system allowing visitors to their website to send an e-card. It's all to do with boosting tourism. There are only eight cards to chose from. But yes, one of them is a big, shiny jar of the mighty-M.

To send it to your friends (or yourself) go to: *www.enjoyeaststaffs.co.uk/postcard*

E-Bay: at any given time there's close to 300 Marmite-related items on the UK site.

Perhaps surprisingly, the US site is also a rich hunting ground for memorabilia hunters.

Empty: an empty jar! For some reason many people seem to have a problem getting at that last bit, that frustrating amount left, tucked away under the neck of the jar. The internet is jammed with people asking how? You'd think they were after gold. Anyway, how hard can it be? Basically, as long as it's you who's going to be eating the last teeny-weeny glob, use your finger!

It's also suggested, in all seriousness, that turning the jar upside down is the best way. But that's a waste of time: the stuff does not move! But if you're totally determined about not wasting a nano-drop, fill the jar with hot water – and have a mug of Marmite. It apparently has puzzled thousands, but it's hardly rocket science.

End-User: in 2007 Microsoft awarded $700,000 in funding to computer science researchers... and the IT world got Marmite! The money went to those who were working towards establishing an 'end-user' programme

– creating an 'open and diverse community of sensor data'. The aim was to develop a 'shared infrastructure and tools for data publishing, management, querying and visualisation' In computer-geek speak this is known as a 'mash-up'. Which is of no help to those who don't inhabit the deep recesses of a computer laboratory. Basically using a 'mash-up' to create an 'end-user' data compilation allows diverse parts of websites to be drawn together, and united into a complete piece of information. So if you are, say, researching a hotel, the same site will automatically display allied details, such as airports, train stations, restaurants, libraries, cinemas, etc.

But the whole point of this entry is that of the 11 projects funded, one of them was called Marmite! Brothers Jason and Jeffrey Wong of the Carnegie Mellon University in Pittsburgh came up with the name via a very logical process. Knowing that Marmite was the end product of putting the left-over **yeast** from the brewing process to good use, they thought that using the name would convey exactly what they we're trying to achieve. Jeff told me: 'Jason came up with the name. He thought it was similar to the edible Marmite. We were scraping up the remains of the Web and putting them into a consumable form.' As for the product that inspired the name, Jeff said he ended up buying a jar to see what it was all about. He had just one word for it: 'Salty!' Jeff also revealed that their form of Marmite had inspired Intel in its development of a similar programme. But, understandably, copyright issues got in the way of keeping the Wong brother's chosen name. It was renamed Mashmaker.

English Patient (The): as a novel *The English Patient* won the 1992 Booker Prize. As a film it captured the 1996 Oscar for best picture. And in both, Marmite gets an honourable mention. A hauntingly romantic and tragic love story, set in the final days of World War II in Italy, Marmite was invoked by author Michael Ondaatje as a way of allowing the shot-down pilot, who is a Hungarian Count, to prove to his British interrogators that he is on their side. Desperate, to show that he is one of 'them', he suggests: 'Ask me about Marmite!' In the movie the context is changed. The nurse (Kristin Scott Thomas) caring for the horribly injured pilot (Ralph Fiennes) is asked by him to name her favourite things. She tells him: 'Water, with fish in it. Hedgehogs. I love hedgehogs. Marmite – I'm addicted to it. Baths, but not with other people.' Of course the fact that Ondaatje uses Marmite in the book underlines how very British Marmite is – and how citizens of the Commonwealth (apart from the Aussies) have always clung onto it as an example of their undying loyalty to the 'mother' country. Ondaatje was born in Sri Lanka (then Ceylon), moved to Britain at age 11, then to Canada eight years later, where he still lives.

Ex-pats: there are many famous ones who

pack their luggage with jars of Marmite to take back to their exotic home locations. But none has been as lyrical as legendary foreign correspondent Robert Fisk. In May 2009, the London *Independent* 'man-in-the-Middle-East' put the problems and conflicts of the troubled region on the back-burner for a day, to pen a tribute to his life-long love of Marmite. Headlined: Wherever I go in the world, the power of Marmite follows me, the article was spread over half a page. In it Robert, who is based in Beirut, admitted: 'I never really discovered why this horrible-looking stuff was so addictive.'

He tracks his reliance on it right back to childhood, through the dark days of his first boarding-school, where it was not served, to his travels around the world where he's failed to convert to local food passions. He recalls his first trip to France, as a schoolboy. 'There was salade de fruits and crêpe fourrée d'oeufs brouillés, ratatouille and galettes – but no bloody Marmite. My sensitive schoolboy stomach – ironed for years with the contents of that odd little glass pot with its silly yellow lid – simply couldn't take saumon fumé or even a plate of chèvre and the ridiculous long loaves that cut my gums when I tried to chew them. The French obviously had no taste. How could they live without Marmite?'

Then he tells the story of how his local cook caught him on the balcony of his Beirut home, eating it. 'I had bought a pot from London. She asked to try it. So I made a small piece of toast, coated it liberally with butter and lashings of Marmite. I found her extracting it from her mouth in horror. "Mr Robert, how can you EAT this?" she demanded.' He was prompted to burst into print about Marmite – as a subject for his Saturday column in the *Independent* – after a chat with an Air France steward. He had lived in England, during which time he fell in love with the pubs, the red buses and Marmite. 'Who said the French had no taste?' he concluded. As for himself he does without the taste of Marmite while travelling around the Middle-East. He told me: 'I don't travel with a jar. Going through airports it can attract unwanted attention...' And he was delighted to learn about the entry under 'D', which involves Lancaster University where he had been a student – long before his 'homesick-cure' food was a subject for serious study.

Decades before Fisk was posted to Beirut the London *Observer* newspaper was represented there by a notorious correspondent and Marmite-fan, Kim **Philby**.

Ex-Pat 2: there probably isn't a jungle, an atoll, a fiord, or remote mountain range, where you won't find a Brit. They're everywhere. And every time a poll is taken to find out what ex-pats miss most about Britain, the number one thing is – a big drum roll, here – Marmite.

Eyes: in the second book of her trilogy, *Ready, Sex, Go*, Kate Cann talks about Marmite-pot eyes. In a glossary (for her non-

British readers) she explains: 'Marmite is a traditional, black, yeasty spread and it comes in a round jar. So, round, deep and black...'

"Darlink... yu 'ave zee must beautiful Marmite eyes."

F

Fantasy: real fans probably have all sorts of titillating fantasies about what to do with Marmite, and with whom! But death by Marmite...? What sort of mind could dwell on such nonsense? Well, that of an *Archers* fan. The BBC runs a website devoted to *The Archers*, the radio-soap that's been running since 1950. One section is for people to reveal their fantasies about life in Ambridge and the characters who populate it. In April 2002, one 'fan' came up with a way to kill-off Jack. Writing under the name 'Mel O'Drama', he or she had Betty (now killed-off in the programme) building a huge display of Marmite jars in the village shop. Delighted with her innovative promotion skills, Betty called Peggy and Jack, the shop's owners, to come and inspect her mountain of Marmite. But they were not impressed. In her desire to push Marmite, Betty had hidden the tea. Peggy, in exasperation, reached out to get at some. Her elbow knocked the stack of Marmite and the whole lot came tumbling down. Both Peggy and Jack were buried and crushed under the onslaught of the black and yellow jars. At Borchester General Hospital 'death by Marmite' was pronounced as the cause. To read the 'fantasy' in full go to: *www.bbc.co.uk/radio4/archers/listeners/fantasies/death_by_marmite*

Ferrets: love racing. Especially if they know they're scurrying towards a favourite treat. Make that Marmite and you'll have a winner on your hands. That's what Dawn Bradfield of Swindon says. And she should know. She and husband Bob stage ferret-racing at summer country fairs throughout Southern England and the Midlands. That's where ferrets are popped in cut-off drain pipes and the first one out of the far end wins. They have eight pet ferrets and they all simply devour Marmite. Dawn told me: 'They love it. It's a bit like the ferret-paste treat you buy in the pet-shop – but the ferrets love Marmite so much more.

And we always take a jar with us when we take them racing.'

The people who operate the website *Better-Fundraising-Ideas.com* have picked-up on Dawn's way of encouraging ferrets to race well. Explaining how ferret-racing works, they advise: 'Use ferret friendly inducements to encourage a quick run through the pipes. Apparently, Marmite on bread soldiers is popular.' (Also, as you will have worked out, never hide a Marmite sarnie down your trousers when attending a country fair!)

First: the first recipes were published in a booklet given away free by the original owners, the Marmite Food Extract Company Ltd. Simply called *Marmite Recipes* it's hard to pin down the exact publication date, as it was undated but it was probably in the early 1920s. The pen and ink sketches illustrating the 24-page pamphlet are certainly of that era. They show a happy family picnicking, with a white tablecloth carefully laid with cups and saucers and thinly cut sandwiches being handed round on a plate; a stern looking doctor in a three-piece suit and wing collar, watching over a subservient Florence Nightingale-style nurse, as they tend to the sick; a housewife in a pretty frilly pinafore, tied at the back with a big bow, taking a steaming casserole out of the oven; a chubby-cheeked, romper-suited toddler in a wooden high-chair; a slice of bread on a very old-fashioned toasting-fork, and women in classic 1920-style fashion being served by waitresses, or maids, in uniforms of those times.

The introduction points out that the recipes explain the many uses to which Marmite can be put – and 'Marmite users will thus be able to introduce it in a hundred other ways, after a little practice.' It goes on to list what are called the 'merits' of Marmite. They're listed as: 'the tempting flavour; its high concentrated nourishing value; its health building properties'. All of which are 'recognised by people in all walks of life'.

As for the recipes... There's a wide range of soups, stews, roasts, vegetarian pies, soufflés, and fish, vegetable, cheese and egg dishes. But some of the recipes and ideas for using Marmite prove that Marmite and the whacky ways of eating it have been around since day one. For example recommended sandwich fillings, along with butter and Marmite, are: thin slices of banana; finely chopped figs, dates or nuts; freshly picked, washed and chopped watercress.

The Cheese Cream is a Marmite lovers dream. A mix of beaten eggs and milk is heated until it thickens, when grated Gruyere or cheddar, with a good dollop of Marmite, is added, before being reheated and poured into custard glasses – and served hot.

And the instructions for making Marmite Cheese Toast just underline that there is really nothing new about how to indulge Marmite fans. Warm toast is spread with

Marmite butter (a mix of three parts butter, one part Marmite) and covered with a layer of grated cheese and grilled until melted.

So while today we (well, some of us) rave about all the Marmite impregnated products on the market, as in rice cakes, crisps, crackers, cashews and bread sticks, there is nothing 'modern' about them. The recipe for Marmite Biscuits is a basic pastry dough, with Marmite mixed into the milk. And as for the Savoury Marmite Fritters, it's amazing they can't be found in the freezer section of all supermarkets, just waiting to be reheated!

A variation on what is commonly known as 'eggy bread' or, in America, French toast, stale slices of bread, either smeared with Marmite or soaked in milk and Marmite, dipped in beaten egg or a light batter, are fried in hot fat until a golden colour.

While the Marmite Food Extract Company was still around, it republished the booklet a couple of times. Each time it added a recipe or two and kept-up with the times by producing the illustrations, first in Marmite livery colours of black and orange, then with full-colour sketches. The second issue, this time entitled *60 Marmite Recipes*, had another fritter recipe. This one was listed under the exotic title of Savoury Milan Fritters. It added cold mashed potato, grated cheese, flour and chopped chives or parsley, to the bread soaked in beaten eggs and Marmite milk. The mixture was moulded into small flat cakes, brushed with beaten egg and rolled in grated cheese, before being fried.

By the time *100 ways of Using Marmite* came out in the mid 1930s the Marmite Company had really got the hang of putting a zing into the still-free publication. It was more of a paperback than a pamphlet, with full colour sketches, not of people, but of meals ready to serve. The style and the customs of those 'flapper' days between the wars were stamped all over it. In the forward it stated that the sketches represented 'an ordinary 8-course dinner'. And sure enough, every table setting showed properly arranged, appropriate cutlery, for soup, fish, meat, salad, desert and cheese. Sorbet and petit fours should probably have been in there somewhere, too. The comments that accompanied the various chapters and individual recipes threw a light on the way certain people conducted their lives, especially the way in which they – or their servants – spent time in the kitchen. For example, the instructions for a Marmite Glaze is written in a tone that indicated the home-cooking of what we now refer to as 'deli-meats' was as normal as putting the kettle on! 'Next time you are glazing a ham or a tongue, try this savoury glaze. You will find your cold meats greatly improved.' The recipe was simplicity itself. Just 1oz of powdered gelatine, ½ pint of boiling water and 1 tablespoon of Marmite. As a adjunct to the Marmite Fritters, it said: 'An appetising addition to the breakfast table. Try it instead of fried bread.'

For 'another addition to the picnic basket' they suggested 'tasty but inexpensive' Mock Crab Sandwiches. The filling was: grated Cheddar, crushed hard-boiled egg, finely chopped tomato, mixed into a paste with mustard and Marmite. The sandwich was built three-tier – with white and brown bread, buttered and spread with Marmite, the brown slice on both sides as it went in the middle (presumably to give a look of the brown meat of crab).

And the good-old, plain-old Marmite sandwich stand-by, was given a twist for those special occasions. 'Try these at your next bridge party, or for that day in the car when you pack your lunch', was the introduction to the suggestion to add finely chopped nuts to thin slices of white or brown bread, spread with butter and you know what. After instructing to trim the crusts, the maker was told to cut in neat shapes. Adding: 'For bridge teas, stamp out with cutters of hearts, diamonds, etc.'

And again, to show that all the 'new' ideas of how to eat it are not really new, how about this for what to do with the aforementioned Marmite Biscuits: 'Make some oval Marmite biscuits. Place on each one a cooked, stoned prune, which has been filled with a mixture made of cream cheese, Marmite butter and a little chopped gherkin. Pipe round each a little Marmite butter. Serve cold, garnished with parsley or cress.'

This publication – the final one by the original company – ended with a page devoted to 'Marmite for Infants and Children'. It made no bones about it: it was good for kids and they should have it every day. Even babies! It said: 'Marmite is highly recommended for children of all ages. And the opinion has been expressed, by doctors and other scientific people, that every child should have a little Marmite daily. Infants who are backward in growth and do not put on weight, often improve rapidly if Marmite is added to their daily diet. Babies take Marmite eagerly in milk, and its addition is very beneficial in counter-acting the tendency to internal sluggishness which an exclusive milk diet so often produces.'

If your appetite has been whetted by these publications, search for them on e-Bay.

Fishing: don't forget to take your Marmite with you when you go for a day casting a line. Not in sandwiches but on your bait! J M Taylor, of Long Stratton, Norfolk, sells a Marmite marinade by the bucketful. He says it's worth spending time soaking the bait in the black stuff because of the difference it makes in reeling in a good haul. Particularly partial to the Mmm-bait, he assures, are carp and catfish.

Endorsing this bizarre use of Marmite is Britain's bait guru and top carp-catcher Tim Richardson. He writes extensively on the subject of bait. In an article, posted September 2007, on *www.searchwarp.com* (that's not a mistake, it's not 'searchcarp', but a writers' website community) titled, How to Make Easy Catfish and Carp Baits – Simple,

Cool Ingredients for Instant Success he suggested buying ready-made mix to make pastry-balls-bait. The sugar, salt, fat and wheat content in the pastry, makes the bait 'pretty addictive', he claims. But to really get them biting, add Marmite. 'You can make the bait that much better by rolling the pastry out and liberally spreading it with yeast extract, like Marmite.'

MARMITE
The fisherman's friend

To be fair, he mentioned peanut butter as an addition before going onto yeast extract, where he also included **Vegemite**. (But... this is a book about Marmite). Then in conversation he emphasised to me how fish not only love Marmite but how it's good for them! 'Marmite is proven not only to trigger feeding, it is also proven to strengthen immunity against micro-organisms in fish such as carp.' Sounds like this angling tip is nothing to carp about – unless you happen to be one!

Folic acid: Marmite is loaded with it. It's also known as folate, and occasionally referred to by its vitamin status, B-9. It's essential for physical well-being, helping to keep red blood cells healthy. It's believed a deficiency of Folic acid can be an underlying cause for many ravaging conditions, including colon cancer, lupus, rheumatoid arthritis and bowel disorders. But one thing is for sure: maintaining a high level of it is crucial during pregnancy. Standard medical practice recommends an increased dosage, particularly during the first 12 weeks, to ensure the good development of the foetus, and protect against spina-bifida and heart defects.

And all this because India was a British colony, Marmite was a staple product demanded by ex-pats and Dr Lucy Wills had the guts in 1928 to take herself off to work in Bombay. Educated at Cheltenham Ladies College, Cambridge and the London School of Medicine, the independently minded Dr Wills journeyed to the sub-continent in a bid to find out whether diet was a factor in pernicious anaemia during pregnancy. After exhaustive research she determined that it was triggered by a vitamin deficiency. So began the search for a supplement that would overcome the deficiency.

All sorts of things were tried, on monkeys and rats. But nothing did the trick. One monkey was really suffering. For reasons which are not recorded in her notes – maybe sheer desperation – Dr Wills fed it some Marmite. The result was startling. The monkey regained its strength and vitality. And thus, by chance, the resourceful doctor broke through a medical mystery.

Expansive research and testing on pregnant women followed. A variety of substances were tried. But it was only the inclusion of Marmite in their diet that worked the magic. In 1933 Dr Wills concluded that it was the effect of some, as yet, 'undetermined factor' that was present in Marmite. It wasn't until 1941 that Folic acid was officially discovered. Until then it was known as the 'Wills factor'.

At the outbreak of World War II, she returned to London and continued her Marmite research, with 500 pregnant women, at the Royal Free Hospital. Later in life, Dr Wills, who never married, served as a Labour councillor for Chelsea. She died in 1964, at the age of 76, knowing that – thanks to her – every mother-to-be was being told by her doctor to dig into the Marmite!

Food: the brewery sludge was a 'food' long before Marmite came into being. Hundreds of years ago, brewers in Belgium hired workers who worked for very little, or were not paid at all. In lieu of wages they were allowed to take home as much of the **yeast** scrapings, left over from the process, as they wanted. So, in turn the sludge was used to feed many a starving family.

Football: Jon Cotterill, a Brit living in Brazil, is doing his bit to spread the word about the spread around the world. As a commentator for TV Globo he has a daily blog about Brazilian 'futubol' that is read in every football crazy country. He introduces himself as: 'A São Paulo-based Marmite eating, brown sauce guzzling, Jonny foreigner.' He hails from Nottingham and moved to Brazil eight years ago after meeting his Brazilian wife while studying at Brighton University. Jon, who eats Marmite daily, told me he is always nervous about running out of his supply. So a condition for his receiving visitors from Britain is that they must bring Marmite! To read his take on the style of football that gave the world Mirandinha go to:
http://pitacodogringo.wordpress.com

Football-2: Chelsea and French international striker Nicolas Anelka is well assimilated into the British way of life. But he still can't cope with Marmite. Just the sight of it puts him off. In May 2008 he told *FourFourTwo* magazine: 'I've seen Marmite but I've never dared taste it.' If he ever gets round to plucking up the courage, it may well supersede porridge when it comes to the list of food he hates. 'The most disgusting thing I've eaten is probably porridge.'

G

Gay: there's a lot of mucky slang around that links gays with the metaphoric use of Marmite; if you like reading that sort of thing you can Google it for yourself.

Gay-2: a memorable TV commercial featured an infamous man-on-man **kiss**. It was hailed by the gay community as a landmark breakthrough in **advertising**.

German: there is a yeast extract made in Germany, **Vitam-R**, manufactured since 1925 in Hamelin, that sells very well in Britain. It's sold under the Essential label. Although it is very similar in taste to Marmite, there is a subtle, but distinct, difference. Its yeast extract comes from the bakery – not the brewery, although the label does not point that out. It also has less salt, and is **organic**, which accounts for its mounting sales. British fans are eagerly awaiting the arrival of the latest variant, Mello. It's Vitam-R with honey and maple syrup. A unique blend of sweet and savoury. There's no obvious reason why the same formula shouldn't work with Marmite... Time will tell if it ever follows the trend set by the yeast extract Pied-Piper of Hamelin...

Gold: although Marmite was not a huge seller when it first came on the market, its value in the kitchen was recognised very early on by top professionals. At the 1903 Cookery and Food Exhibition, held in Britain's most prestigious exhibition space of the day, London's Albert Hall, it was awarded a Gold Medal.

Gold-2: to mark Marmite's 100th year – in 2002 – the 260 employees at the **Burton-on-Trent** factory all received limited edition gold jars in a commemorative box. Occasionally you can find one being sold on e-Bay.

The Duke of Edinburgh also received the special birthday gift pack. To mark Marmite's centenary year he toured the Burton-on-Trent factory. But his commemorative present also included a gold toast rack.

Gourmet: OK, perhaps this is going too far! Unless you are using common nouns. Yes, 'gourmet' and 'marmite', as in the French cooking pot, could feasibly be used in the same sentence, or breath. But 'gourmet' and 'Marmite'? No way. Mentioning them side by side amounts to a total oxymoron. But spell 'gourmet' with a capital 'G' and that's a whole different matter.

It's a splendid connection, because then we're talking about *Gourmet*, the American food magazine which is a monthly must-read for foodies, for whom life without fine food is not worth living. An attitude that is shared – as you would imagine – by the magazine's staff, including copy chief John Haney. He spends his working day pouring over articles about the eating and preparation of exquisite cuisine, reading submissions about travelling the world in search of gourmet experiences.

But to ready himself for this arduous business he starts his day with Marmite...

The kitchen in his Brooklyn Heights, New York, apartment is never without it. But then John, born in 1954, is an Essex boy, from Romford. And he's immortalised the pivotal place Marmite has always had in his life in a wonderful book: *Fair Shares for All – a Memoir of Family and Food*, an honourable mention is given to Marmite four times.

The book grew from a piece John wrote for the January 2003 *Gourmet*, in which 'memories that nourish the working-class soul of a transplanted Englishman', were evoked. The article hit a nerve with a New York literary agent, who encouraged John to expand it into a book. The result? An enormously entertaining and evocative read.

The first Marmite mention in the book is when John is recalling the wondrous tea-times he spent at his grandparents. '...doorsteps, painted with Marmite, an incredibly salty, **yeast**-based spread that is guaranteed to horrify anyone who didn't acquire a taste for it within a couple of years of leaving the womb...' He was obliged to explain Marmite because *Fair Shares for All* was published in America. Bafflingly, it's never found a British publisher. It is, however, available via Amazon's UK site.

Gout: if you suffer from what some consider the most painful chronic medical condition known to man – and, increasingly to woman –

and you consume Marmite regularly, there is bad news. It may be the cause, or at least contributing to it. Because it contains high levels of purine, and **niacin**, it is pin-pointed as a 'no-no', with all other yeast extracts, for those desperate to keep gout at bay.

Guantanamo: a grim place but it's been used in black humour to highlight just how some people can't stand Marmite: how just being in the same room as a jar brings them out in a cold sweat. Guantanamo Bay and Marmite were brought together in an article that was published on *The Spoof* website. Posted material – which is contributed by spoof-merchants from around the world – is exactly what the site name indicates: fictitious, totally untrue and a parody on the harsh and hilarious realities of life. The piece, written under the pseudonym of Roy Turse (say it quickly), 'revealed' how Marmite was being used as a weapon of torture against prisoners held at Guantanamo Bay. The torturers were wielding it under the noses of prisoners, force-feeding them with it, although the use of Marmite was banned under the Geneva Convention, as cruel and unusual punishment. The whacky posting went on: 'Although any information recovered using Marmite would not be admissible in court, the effectiveness of it for extracting information is not debated. Known as the "truth spread" in parts of the Middle East, just the rumour that there is a jar of Marmite on the premises is enough to strike fear into the hearts of detainees.'

The author, owner of a networking equipment company in Hitchin, Hertfordshire, (who wants to stay anonymous in case he writes professionally one day) knows of what he writes. 'I'm a bit of a fan of Marmite,' he confessed to me. 'But my wife and children are in the "hate" camp.' Being the rotter he is, when it comes to stirring up tortuous Marmite plots, it doesn't stop him stirring it into stews and casseroles when it's his turn to cook. To read the full version of his cruel take on Marmite go to: *www.thespoof.com* where you will also find at least nine other postings involving Marmite.

Guinness: you probably expect to read here about the Guinness-Marmite limited edition collaboration (that's mentioned next). No, the really good story (apart from another further down) featuring Guinness is the one about Steven Guinness. He is a true Mr Marmite. It's his eating habits – no, make that 'habit' – that earned him the title. Since he was a toddler, Steven has consumed virtually nothing but Marmite. Apart from various types of bread, a few chips now and then, an occasional apple and some honey, that is all he eats! He drinks only Ribena or water. Never tea or coffee – not even hot Marmite as a drink. Occasionally he might have a glass of wine when he's out with his pals. And if they go out to grab a bite, he'll have some chips. And that's it.

'Marmite is something I literally cannot live without,' Steven, from Ainsdale, near Southport, Lancashire, told the *Daily Express* in July 2007. Now, 24, nothing has changed. Breakfast, lunch and dinner, are all the same. Marmite on toast, on a bread-bun, on a baguette. And not just smeared. Thick, thick, thick. As his mother Carol, with whom he lives, told told me: 'It's an eye-watering sight.' Her older son, Jonathan, 27, who also lives with her, eats properly. Like her he enjoys Marmite occasionally but eaten, as Carol explains with a laugh, 'in a normal way.'

She and Steven's late father used to worry constantly about Steven's Marmite-only diet. 'At first, as a child, he could not tolerate anything else. He would bring it back, regurgitate it, immediately.' For many years Steven – who is a lean 5' 10" and works in an Oxfam shop – underwent constant medical attention. He was always being seen by doctors – tested, examined, probed. But they could not pin-point a problem. No condition was diagnosed. When he turned 14, the year his father died, Steven announced he was fed-up with their attention and refused to be seen by any more doctors. Carol added: 'At the beginning he had the problem of keeping food down. Now he just isn't interested in eating anything else. But he's healthy, full of energy and perfectly well.'

As for the special edition of Marmite and his namesake (see next entry), what did Steven think of that? 'He didn't like it,' reported his mother. 'He said it had a different taste.' What about all the Marmite infused goodies available now? Forget it. He hates the crisps, the rice-cakes, cheese and bread-sticks. But Carol says: 'I've stopped worrying about him – and he's easy and cheap to cater for!'

Guinness-2: In early 2007 the first special-edition of Marmite rolled off the production line. It was the merging of Marmite and Guinness – and the collaboration was to mark March 17, St Patrick's Day. Only 30% of the yeast extract came from the vast vat of Guinness waste. Unlike the original **Guinness Yeast extract** spread (see next entry). And despite all the promotional work that went into launching the special edition, no mention was ever made that Guinness had once produced its own version. Like the other special editions (**champagne** and **cricket-**ball) samples from an exhaustive supply – of the 300,000 jars of Marmite-Guinness produced – are still available. On e-Bay, of course. Even an empty jar becomes a highly prized souvenir.

Guinness Yeast Extract (GYE): in the early 1900s Guinness decided that they would challenge Marmite. If the original was made from the left-over **yeast** sludge from common-or-garden British beer, imagine how good an alternative product would be if the starter-yeast came from Guinness...

They already had a by-product – drying surplus yeast and selling it as animal feed. So Guinness instructed its then chief chemist, Dr James Hill Millar, to experiment with processing a yeast extract that would be both fit for human consumption and palatable. A 'tonic' was what Guinness first had in mind.

By 1920 Dr Millar was making progress, having come up with a pressed-yeast that was soluble. Market research for such a 'tonic' product was encouraging. But it took more than another decade before Guinness was ready to go public with both the pressed-yeast and a spread. Finally, on November 2 1936, *GYE* – Guinness Yeast Extract – hit the shops. But a major hurdle – 'patent restrictions' – prevented its being sold in mainland Britain, or even in Northern Ireland. Marmite, clearly, was not going to allow the rival from across the Irish Sea to invade British territory. Even so, GYE boomed. Production, in Dublin, started at a ton a day. Its popularity was helped by the publication, in 1946, of the *GYE Recipe Book*. By 1950 weekly production had expanded to 12 tons.

But in 1968 Guinness conceded defeat and it was discontinued. Folk-lore has it that many a jar of GYE was found years later in Irish kitchens, devotees having stocked-up before it was too late. Bearing in mind Guinness' foray into the yeast extract market, what irony, then, that it forged a relationship with Marmite in 2007 to mark St Patrick's Day, producing those 300,000 jars of Guinness-laced Marmite. Strangely, in the talks to set up the collaboration there was no mention of GYE. No chatter, reminiscing about the once-upon-a-time rivalry? Hard to believe, but that's what Guinness told me.

The 1946 cookery book, to promote Guinness'

yeast extract spread, was written by the wonderfully named Mrs D. D. Cottington-Taylor. The cover of the book listed her impressive resume. She started her professional life armed with a certificate in Household and Social Sciences from King's College for Women, followed by First Class Teaching Diplomas in Cookery, Laundrywork, Housewifery and High-class Cookery.

Her credentials, plus being the author of many other cookery books, had led this post-war Mrs Beeton to the lofty position of being the first Director of the newly-formed Good Housekeeping Institute. It was under that title she penned the GYE book, although the biggest name on the cover was that of the publisher: Arthur Guinness, Son & Company Ltd. The book was to introduce GYE in 'simple everyday cooking recipes' as 'formulated' by the good Mrs Cottington-Taylor.

Good Housekeeping told me that she had clearly been a 'formidable' woman and that she would be getting a special mention in the book, due to be published in 2010, to commemorate the centenary of the National Magazine Company, of which *Good Housekeeping* was a founding publication.

Meanwhile the *GYE Recipe Book* – a copy of which is on display in the Guinness Storehouse (its Dublin museum) – is very much in the collector's realm. Anyone who has one needs to know it is metaphorically stamped 'rare' and should immediately put it under lock and key!

"Any advance on this Marmite-like treasure..."

H

Hangovers: many swear that Marmite is the answer to a hangover. There are lots of tales to back up the theory, which is founded on an intake of lashings of Vitamin-B quickly restoring the body with many of the essential vitamins that are stripped out by indulging in alcohol. In Sri Lanka a popular pick-me-up after a session is a revolting sounding concoction of boiling water, lime juice, Marmite and fried onions. It must be so obnoxious to swallow, that the hangover is probably taken over by feeling totally unwell.

But in December, 2008 – just in time for the Christmas and New Year bender season – the *British Medical Journal* carried an article that quashed the yeast extract cure. Drs Rachel

Vreeman and Aaron Carroll concluded that, after extensive review, searching for a potion to bang a hangover on the head was pointless. 'There is no scientific evidence' they declared. And this sad statement was made after having researched the impact on sufferers of many claimed cures. From aspirin and bananas, to yeast extract spread mixed in water.

But maybe there is a glimmer of hope for Marmite in this arena. The two doctors who gave the thumbs down to yeast extract are American! And they actually cited Vegemite in their study. And, as everyone who knows anything about the product under discussion, there's a world of difference between the two... So, you believers, keep on supping the Marmite, after you've supped too much. Maybe that vital something, that makes Marmite and Vegemite so different, will make all the difference to that hangover.

Holidays: huge number of Brits can't leave home without it. According to the official Marmite website, 25% of holiday-makers take a jar with them. If you're in that category, and you're flying, remember two things: under the gels/creams/lotions/liquids restriction, you cannot take it in your carry-on (unless you're so desperate to keep up your daily intake and you're only going on an overnight trip, you decant it into a teeny-container holding a mere 100 ml); and while it is safe to check in your luggage (despite some silly talk on the internet that says it will implode no matter what the conditions) best to wrap it in something leak-proof, as you should any other non-solid item just in case the plane loses pressure.

"Sorry sir, I don't care if it is just full of Marmite... it's still excess baggage!"

Hooch: HM prisoners love Marmite. Sometimes they even eat it! They're also very fond of trying to take it back to its alcoholic beginnings. A common misconception is that because of its high **yeast** content it makes an excellent fermenting aid. And by the time the jailbirds add fruit and veg, stolen from the prison kitchen, they're confident they've got a vaguely drinkable hooch.

In January 2002 Marmite was claimed to be the basis of cell-made booze at Featherstone jail, near Wolverhampton. The annual report by the prison's Board of Visitors revealed the sandwich-spread trick. Then in March 2007 a riot at Edmunds Hill jail, near Stradishall, Suffolk, was blamed on Marmite based alcohol. So on that basis you'd think that Marmite would be off the menu in HM prisons? But no way. Because, as a spokesperson for HM Prisons told me: 'The ingredients for Marmite do not include any active yeast and as such it is impossible to use Marmite in the production of alcoholic beverages.' So there, all you old and young lags – you may as well use the Marmite you get in prison to put on your porridge. Like they're very fond of doing in Malaysia.

Hopkins: in 1912 biochemist Frederick Gowland Hopkins published a scientific paper that gave Marmite – then 10 years old – a massive marketing boost. It had a desperately complicated name: *Feeding Experiments Illustrating the Important of Accessory Food factors in Normal Dietaries,* but it packed a powerful punch. It not only opened the way to the discovery of vitamins but very quickly established how **yeast** held the key to many of them, particularly the vital Bs.

It was confirmation for what the Marmite owners had always suspected: that Marmite was a health giving product. In 1925 Hopkins was knighted and in 1929 he was awarded the Nobel Prize for Medicine and Physiology, for his ground-breaking work with 'trace substances' – the original name for vitamins.

Horror: many people have a Marmite horror anecdote. Some revolve around offering, usually unsuspecting foreigners, luscious looking chocolate spread, slathered on crackers; or smearing it on bed sheets to shock chambermaids; or pasting it on lavatory flush handles to spook out house-mates.

There can be few families in the land without a Marmite tale to tell. Mine is quite simple but totally memorable and still makes me laugh and my brother Martin wince. Mother was putting a picnic lunch together, in the beach chalet we'd rented. Most of the family – grown-up kids and little kids – were on the sands, waiting for the 'grub up' summons. Except aforementioned bro, who was lounging in a deckchair, reading the paper. My job was to set out the food, ready for the hungry hoard to descend. I took out a plate of open-faced baps, smeared in Marmite. I returned a minute later, this time with a plate of baps adorned with ham, to find the first plate almost demolished. 'Oh, no!' was my cry. To which Martin muttered, with his mouth still full: 'Good heavens, so what - I've started before everyone is here. What's the problem?' I had barely stammered out 'but that's Marmite not **Bovril**' before he was up on his feet, his face showing all the signs of a man about to throw up. He doesn't hate much in life. But Marmite was top of that short list. Or, so he'd thought...

Hors d'oeuvre: mushrooms, sautéed in Marmite! Served on thick, crusty toast. What a perfect starter to set before any Marmite-lover. And those living in, staying in, or passing through the delightful village of Stockbridge, Hampshire, can so easily get such a treat. All they have to do is pop into the White Hart Inn, in the High Street, where Marmite Mushrooms is on the 'starters and small plates' menu. Christopher Masters, manager of the 12th Century inn, came up with the idea when he was looking for something a bit different in pub food. At first he put the £4.75 Marmite creation only on the Autumn-Winter menu. But regulars made such a clamour about the dish disappearing over the spring and summer, it's now on year-round. Assistant manager Jackie Higgs tells me: 'It's one of our signature dishes. We get a lot of comments about it. We also hear a lot of giggles when people are reading the menu. We also have some staff who when they're serving it say, oh, I can't stand the smell of it. I just tell them, how can you not love Marmite?'

I

Ice-Cubes: made from a lot of Marmite stirred into a little water, dropped into a Bloody Mary (see **Cocktails**), will make you the cleverest cocktail-maker and shaker around. Also they work well in the picnic gazpacho, to keep it cool and add flavour. And they could be the absolute answer to the pregnant whose cravings see them crunching ice-cubes, while eating Marmite straight from the jar.

Independent: an avalanche of letters and e-mails, all about Marmite, deluged the newspaper in 2006. The letter-writing storm was sparked by a feature about the new *VideoJug* website that gave instructions on how to do everyday things properly. The article repeated, word for word, the instructions for such simplistic tasks as tying a tie, flossing teeth, folding a shirt and how to make Marmite on toast. For the latter the instructions were: 'spread a generous helping of Marmite over the butter...' Fairly innocuous, one might think.

But the *Independent* mail-room was hit by a tidal wave of thoughts and opinions about Marmite to such an extent that, three weeks later, the paper ran another feature about the anger, protests and horror that the original one triggered. The basic dispute was over the way in which the instructions called for a 'generous' amount of Marmite, but it rapidly descended (some one would say rose) into an all embracing Marmite outpouring, of thoughts, comments, trivia, personal and historic information.

The second story told readers that hundreds of letters and e-mails had swamped the *Independent*. All this, at a time when the country was struggling with the war in Iraq; global warming warnings; Tony Blair's departure date as Prime Minister; policy towards Muslims; rising house-prices; immigration and a prison crisis. The piece pointed out: 'Before you could say "hell-in-a-handcart", people were talking about "the end of civilisation as we know it". Who would have thought such a subject, lacking meat as it is in every respect, could unleash such a bilious torrent?'

Every day, from August 31 (the day after the offending article) until October 14, there was at least one Marmite letter printed. One of the most illuminating was from a café owner in Redcar, Cleveland. He wrote: 'In my café I have long felt that Marmite is not everyone's cup of tea. I offer my customers "Marmite Sandwiches – without the Marmite". These are very popular.'

Insects: book-binder Mark Cockram, of Barnes, London, banked on beetles loving Marmite… He planned to take part in the 2009 *Pestival* – an intra-media exhibition glorifying insects – with his *Big Book of Marmite and Bugs*. Before binding the pages, he soaked them in a solution of diluted Marmite. They turned a deep champagne beige. He then printed on them using an 'ink' which took its tint from a darker solution of Marmite.

At the three-day 'Pestival', in September, at London's Southbank Centre, the book – with its title written with a squeezy-jar of Marmite – was due to be exhibited alongside a film of its making. A colony of skin beetles (proper name: *dermestes maculatus*) were to be released into the book, and visitors would watch as they nibbled their way, artistically, through the pages!

But Lincoln-born Mark, who has studied his craft in Britain and Tokyo, and teaches and exhibits all over the world, took some flak from other book-binders. He told me: 'As a classically trained book-binder and restorer, the idea of making a book to be destroyed goes against the grain. Comments from some

of my fellow book-binders have likened it to book burning. The flip side of this, of course, is that as a book artist it is important to step out of the comfort zone and push to breaking point.' As for Marmite? Yes, he loves it. And when he's not using it to dye paper he eats it! To check on Mark's Marmite book, and his other work go to:
www.studio5bookbindingandarts.blogspot.com

Internet: in 1997, when I first had the idea for a Marmite book, there were 523 references to it that could be accessed via a computer. It wasn't the 'internet': nowhere close. It was a data-bank newspapers subscribed to, and a journalist pal did some research for me. I don't remember that figure because of my extraordinary memory but I can just make out a scribble, recording the fact, in a fading note-book. Enter 'Marmite' into a search engine now and wow! In the summer of 2009 there were 'about' 433,000 entries. Torment your Aussie pals with that soaring fact. Only 118,000 entries came up for **Vegemite**. So, just to pick another household name (not entirely at random), how about **Guinness**? That comes up more than three million. Well, who's counting?

Inventions: if you have an idea or invention involving Marmite you are not alone! For an insight into some of the more whacky Marmite concepts, go to: *www.halfbakery.com*. This site is an Aladdin's Cave of inventive and bizarre suggestions for everything you can possibly think of. A compelling site for discovering the wonderful weird thoughts and plans people have for everyday items and procedures. Among the Marmite proposals: deodorant type roller-ball applicator; spray on jar; rice-paper.

Itch: horses frequently suffer an uncomfortable itch (all to do with biting midges) that revels under the bizarre name of sweet-itch. Many owners turn to Marmite to cure it. But just like humans, Marmite only does good to those who can bear to eat it. Judging by the message-boards on various websites, if the inflicted horse doesn't spit it out, then the Marmite – mixed into oats, or just as a sandwich – seems to work wonders.

J

Jardox: ever wondered where the other British yeast extracts (see 'A') come from? As the formula for Marmite is a top-food-processing secret, it's not easy to churn out the replicas. But Jardox, in Sevenoaks, Kent, holds the key to what turns beer yeast waste into an edible form. Established in 1909, the company is the country's leading manufacturer of savoury products, serving food manufacturers and major retailers. Among its wide range is yeast extract – the main ingredient of Marmite. It makes several 'own brands' for leading supermarkets, including Tesco and Asda. It also makes

Natex, a salt-reduced yeast extract spread, that is available from health food shops. It used to manufacture Toastmate, the ill-fated low-salt spread sold under the name of celebrity chef, **Antony Worrall Thompson**

Jesus: Is there no part of life Marmite is not capable of infiltrating? In May 2009, Claire Allen, of Ystrad, in Wales, was making Marmite sandwiches for her three sons when she put the lid on the kitchen counter and let out a cry. She looked at it. She studied it. Then without saying anything she showed the inside of the lid to her oldest son, Jamie, 14. Without any prompting from her, he said: 'That looks like Jesus.' Thanks to her father taking a photograph and giving it to the local paper, the Marmite-Messiah story went round the world, quicker than saying My Mate Messiah. The effect was huge. 'First I couldn't believe what I saw, then I couldn't believe the reaction,' Claire – who is not a church-goer – told me. And it was weeks before she and her husband Gareth and their children could leave home without people stopping them to talk about the image in the lid. And they became weary of denying the rumour that they had sold it for £30,000. 'It's in the fridge,' laughed Claire. 'And that's where it's going to stay.' If nothing else the Jesus-in-the-Lid yarn provided wonderful proof that Marmite and the attitude it invokes is totally global. The first comment left on the *Daily Mail* website about the story was posted by Halina Lahti, of Utena, Lithuania. It read: 'Shows Marmite appeal is everywhere. But the question is does He "loveth it or hateth it"?'

Jerseys: yes, that was a Marmite jar you saw whizzing down the street, or labouring up a mountainside, astride a bike! Foska, a company that specialises in creating practical but witty gear for cyclists, is fond of using household trademarks. The Marmite logo, which they use under licence from **Unilever**, has proved to be a huge seller. Particularly popular is the jersey that teases motorists, as the rider weaves in and around traffic. In a Marmite-style font and colours it declares, on the back: *Hate Jams*.

Jewellery: fancy a bracelet made of tiny ceramic Marmite jars? Maybe a brooch, earrings, pendant, cufflinks, key-ring… even a watch or bookmark, all announcing where the owner stands on the love-loath debate, in the most unique way? The Marmite likeness in each piece is hand-crafted in polymer clay then hand-painted. At least two artists are producing these wearable, useful, creations. Rachel Sherman sells on: *www.etsy.com* (a buying and selling website devoted to hand-made items) and on: *www.mixedupdolly.co.uk*, her own website. Katie Hunt's work can be found on e-bay.

Rachel, of Wells, Somerset, has been making food and confectionary inspired jewellery for 15 years. Her business started when she made a ring for a Marmite-addict friend. This led to lots of requests for similar items and also for other brand product identities, such as Starbuck's, Kit-Kat, Smarties and Guinness. 'But Marmite are my best-selling products,' she happily reports. 'I sell them worldwide and have lots of people who buy them for home-sick, ex-pat relatives, particularly in the States and Australia. I even sell to people who are buying them for friends and relatives who hate Marmite! ' She's currently working on the design for a Marmite clock and Marmite watch. Katie, from Bristol, has the same Marmite success story to tell. 'I've sold plenty of my Marmite jewellery to men, women and children, not only in Britain, but around the world. The feedback is amazing.'

Joke: The kids are helping out in the kitchen, preparing breakfast for their parents. The conversation goes like this:

'Does anyone know what dad wants on his toast?'

'Ma might.'

'Marmite?'
'No, ma might know.'
'No Marmite, then? Ok, he can have jam.'

Joke-2: and, of course, the oldest one of all:
 Knock, knock.
 Who's there?
 Marmite.
 Marmite who?
 Marmite, but Pa won't.

It's funny, if you're a kid and you're in the playground and you've never heard it before. And see **Parwill** for a variation of the joke that ended up as the name for a jar of yeast extract.

(If your sense of humour tends towards the lavatorial, you'll probably want to look under **Poo**...)

June: the 13th should be declared Marvellous Marmite Day. That was the day, in 1902, the Marmite Company came into being. Imagine the fun! Throw a summer party with a Marmite menu. All manner of Marmite ways to 'enhance' conventional dishes and drinks can be found in various entries... even including creative ways to present a Marmite birthday cake!

K

Keswick: the worthy citizens of this charming Lake District town probably see-off their fair share of Marmite. But this reference to Keswick is three thousand miles away in the heart of Greenwich Village, New York. Marmite Central in Manhattan is Myers of Keswick. Each day they make and sell the best pork-pies this side of, well just about anywhere. And they can hardly keep up with the demand for Marmite from British ex-pats who cannot curb their need for that taste of childhood.

The owner of the shop, Pete Myers, knows how to produce a fabulous pork-pie because he grew up in a family of butchers. When love stopped him in his tracks in New York (it was a girl, not the city) and he decided to stay, he had to think of something to do, so he drew on all he knew about making stand pies. Now more than 30 years on, his shop is a Mecca and an institution for those who, despite New York's culinary delights, still cannot cope without a taste of the old country. Even those on short visits beat a path to the shop.

Over the decades he's looked after the pork-pie and Marmite needs of many a famed Brit. One Marmite-run still has him in stitches. But then the late Benny Hill was involved. The funny-man sent his American chauffeur on the mission. The assistant who served him could not understand him, as he struggled to pronounce 'marmite'. Finally he could tell that the assistant was losing patience. 'Don't you know who I'm here for?' he said pompously. Caroline, the assistant, had no idea. But when she heard the name Benny Hill, her feminist beliefs came to the fore. 'If I'd known that I wouldn't have served you!' she snapped.

Kiss: over the generations, kissing has been an integral part of Marmite's eclectic **advertising**. In 1951, *Punch* carried an almost risqué advert – for its time. It showed a newly married man, seated at the dining table, grabbing his bride's bottom as she's about to serve him coffee.

'I want to kiss the new cook!' the copy exclaims. With coffee tray shuddering, and pretty pinafore floating, she giggles: 'Well, you can't, she's busy.' He tells her: 'Come along! Husband's orders!' Then, while calling her 'Mrs Beginner', asks her to what she ascribes her immediate success as a cook? 'To my mother, Sir – and to Marmite.'

Kiss-2: the infamous 'Lifeguard Kiss' commercial, aired in 2003, showed a lifeguard munching on a Marmite and cheese sandwich just moments before dragging a drowning man out of the surf. He gives him the kiss-of-life but as he stops the now-recovered swimmer drags the lifeguard back to him and starts snogging him intently.

Most viewers roared with laughter. They knew it was all about the lure of Marmite proving more powerful than heterosexuality.

Gay and lesbian groups, on both sides of the Atlantic, hailed it as a breakthrough. At last, a same-sex kiss being central to an advertising campaign. They rejoiced. But of course there were those who were deeply troubled. And 71 of them actually sat down and put pen to paper, or fingers to keyboard, and complained to the Advertising Standards Authority, which in turn ruled that the Marmite-kiss – gay or just for the taste of it – was 'not offensive'. In a statement about the commercial, Datamonitor, the global business information and market analysis company, had no doubt that Marmite had hit an **advertising** bull's-eye, while staying true to itself. It said: 'A cult brand such as Marmite knows its target market and is not worried about alienating certain consumers in its marketing messages.

'The Marmite brand has always been up-front and honest about realising some people dislike the taste of the product. This latest tongue in cheek promotion will only add to the immense character and subsequent consumer appeal that the brand has developed over the years.'

Knowledge: if your interest in Marmite, or yeast extract generally, goes way beyond just eating it, there is an organisation just for you.

EURASYP – the European Association for Speciality Yeast Products – is a mine of information, for the technically and scientifically minded. Based in Paris, its website, *www.eurasyp.org*, is in both French and English.

Kosher: only the Marmite made in South Africa, under licence for **Unilever**, passes the true Kosher test. It's all a bit hard to understand, especially as Kosher certification for Marmite goes back to its very earliest days. In 1902 the London Beth Din, the Jewish authority that determines what is and what is not Kosher, sanctioned Marmite. A letter from Chief Rabbi Hermann Adler confirmed this. But over the years there have been concerns about a heating pipeline in the factory in **Burton-on-Trent**. It supplies heating for both the processing of Marmite and **Bovril**. But although neither product has any contact at any stage of production, this pipeline gets in the way of Marmite being granted full Kosher status. And to this day it carries the damning rider: 'not manufactured under Rabbinical Supervision'. The grocery store Just Kosher, in Boreham Wood, North London, confirms that British Marmite is a no-no. And for Jewish fans, like most stores that cater to the orthodox, they always have plenty of Marmite from South Africa in stock. It's easy to tell if you have your hands on the South African version –apart from saying it's made there – the label also carries the appropriate Kosher symbol.

Kut: in the First World War the Mesopotamia (now Iraqi) town of Kut came under siege. A combined Commonwealth force –British, Australian, New Zealand and Indian soldiers – desperate to defend the oil-strategic river junction, had been cut-off by a German-led Turkish force. Supply lines were blocked; rations were down to starvation levels; disease – beriberi, dysentery, scurvy, malaria – was taking its toll. Faced with a humanitarian dilemma of massive proportions, the decision was taken to do something that had never happened before: drop vital supplies and equipment from the air. Included in the air-drop was a vast quantity of Marmite. It was hoped that its concentrated forms of all the health-restoring B-vitamins would save lives, and that the supply drop generally would allow the Brits to hang in and save Kut.

While the Marmite certainly allowed many men to survive, the historic air-drop did not save Kut. Several weeks later, on April 29, 1916, the five-month siege ended with the British surrender. The death-toll was enormous: about 1,750 men died during the siege. Thousands died after being marched away into captivity.

After the war Colonel J Bruce-Kingsmill, who served in III Division in Mesopotamia, wrote a letter in which he praised the help and health Marmite bestowed on his starving and diseased men. 'I have great pleasure in testifying to the excellent results which were brought about by the use of Marmite in Mesopotamia during the war. In cases of beriberi, dysentery, 'Baghdad boils', fever and nephritis (inflammation of the kidneys) it appeared to have a 'vitalising' affect upon the troops, enabling them to produce a more sustained effort during the arduous operations which took place in that broiling sun.'

L

Laura: teen British tennis star Laura Robson let the country affinity cat out of the yeast extract bag, when she competed in the 2009 Australian Open. Australian-born of British parents, she left Melbourne when she was 18-months-old, to spend the next five years in Singapore before coming to live in Britain. But she still has family in Australia, with an aunt and uncle in Western Australia and a sister in Melbourne. So little wonder the Aussies would like to claim her as their own. And bless her heart she fell into the trap during the mandatory press-conference after her first-round victory. Without warning there was the big-test question: did she prefer Marmite or **Vegemite**? The answer came popping out. 'Vegemite,' she said. Which prompted a gleeful response from an Aussie journalist: 'She's an Aussie,' he cried.

Left-Bank: even in the heart of bohemian, arty Paris, Marmite fiends are not neglected.

Have breakfast in the Michelin one-star restaurant at L'Hotel, and smear or cover your croissant with it. L'Hotel might be a true Parisian gem but Marmite is served automatically.

But then the luxury boutique hotel, at 13 rue des Beaux-Arts, has another distinctive feature... It is British owned. Part of the luxury A Curious Group of Hotels it is patronised by high-celebrity French and international 'A' list guests, particularly those from the fashion world, designers and models. The *Financial Times* has called it the fashionistas' favourite place to stay in Paris. Chairman and co-founder of the Oxford-based hotel group, Peter Frankopan, told me why Marmite was introduced at this 'very Parisian little gem', as it has been labelled.

"Non! Non! Marmite.."

'When we bought the hotel in 2005 we were keen to accentuate all that is good about

Great Britain. And, of course, Marmite was one key touch which we thought was both quirky and reflective of whom we are as owners.' He added: 'We now have a new group of Marmite devotees among our A-list clientele, especially American and French, who have become converted after staying or having breakfast meetings at L'Hotel.'

Lids: they started out as cork plugs, atop the original white earthenware white jars. Then when glass jar were introduced the lids were yellow and red metal, with the name on. All hell broke out, in 1984, when the metal lid was replaced with solid yellow plastic, with no writing on. Hard to understand the shock, horror that greeted that change. Many would categorise it as a total-over-the-top reaction. But it underlines the extraordinary passion the true Marmite aficionado feels for it.

Lids-2: despite the outcry over the above change, the silver-lid has been embraced as the ultimate gift for a Marmite lover. The original ones were the creation of maverick jewellery designer Theo Fennell who launched them in 1997. They've been a huge seller ever since. In Sterling silver, they come in 125g and 500g sizes. And a rare find now would be one to fit a 57g jar. Both the lid and the jar are collectibles as, in 2006, Marmite did away with the tiny jar. He also produces exclusive 250g versions. But only to go atop a very limited number of the special editions. As in the 50 he made, engraved with a heart, to go with the Marmite-Champagne as a special commission for Selfridges. They sold for £145 each. Now there's love for you!

Since Fennell failed to get a patent on his Marmite concept plenty of other silversmiths have followed his idea. Among them and racking-up huge sales, with silver-plated lids, is Silver Editions of Chalfont St Peter, Buckinghamshire. The family firm, founded in 1908, started producing £15 Marmite lids in 2004. It fills the gap left by Theo Fennell, because it only makes them in the 250gram size. In mid-2009 they started producing them in sterling, for £55. Although the lids are just a small part of Silver Editions extensive range of silverware, owner Kim Roberts told me: 'A day never goes by that we don't get a Marmite order.' Many of them go overseas, particularly to the land of **Vegemite**, Australia! Also a big seller is the £25 'survival kit' - a 250gram jar of Marmite, a silver-plated lid and spreading knife, packed in an aluminium carrying case.

You'd think that, as it buys Marmite 1,000 jars a time, Silver Editions would get a bit of a discount from owners Unilever. But no: the Marmite-makers refused its request for a break on the price. So Kim approached his local Waitrose – which was only too happy to oblige.

Literature: many authors, over many years, have introduced Marmite into their novels. John Le Carre and Graham Greene gave it an honourable mention, while Joanne Trollope likes her characters feasting on it, as does

Kate Atkinson. But particularly fond of weaving it into his dark humour and satirical writing, is T Coraghessan Boyle. His use of it is even more interesting because he is American. He gives it a pivotal place in *The Miracle of Ballinspittle*, one of his stories in his highly acclaimed *If the River Was Whiskey* collection. The plot revolves around an Irish teenager, Nuala Nolan who, to mark Lent, eats and drinks nothing but Marmite and soda water. After three weeks she sees the hand of a statue of the Virgin Mary move. Word gets out and her small village is flooded with pilgrims. From that day on she never strays from her Marmite-only intake '...until the very synapses of her brain have become encrusted with salt and she raves like a mariner lost at sea...'

Not a hard image for the famed author to conjure up. He is, to put it mildly, not a fan of Marmite. He told me: 'I first tasted the horrible stuff as a hippie with an unrefined palate, circa 1977, in London. My lifetime consumption will fill a very small tumbler, perhaps even a thimble.' And he has his own idea of how Marmite is best eaten. 'Keep those recipes rolling... like Marmite and mud, Marmite and stewed weeds!'

Surprisingly another American novelist has used Marmite in a quirky way. In *The Lamb: the Gospel According to Bif, Christ's Childhood Pal*, Christopher Moore invents his own books of the Bible, like *Excretions, Damnations* and *Amphibians*. And he has two bands of warriors battling each other. He calls them Marmites and Vegemites and they keep 'smiting' each other. 'I know what they both look like and I've tasted Marmite,' he told me. 'I've had a number of people from the UK and Australia mention the reference, but not one American in seven years since the book came out. I'm not sure many Americans know what either one of those things is. I do, however, and I thought it would be a funny "Biblical" sounding reference.'

Loveline: got a question about Marmite, want to settle an argument about Marmite, or just want to tell the Marmite people how you feel about it? There's an easy way. The invitation is on every jar: 'Questions? Call the Marmite loveline free on 0800 0323 656'. The disappointment is that the person who answers doesn't mention 'love'! It's the 'care line'. And if whoever takes the call isn't careful they might forget the 'Marmite' bit! Because the person who answers is not a dedicated Marmite specialist. All calls about **Unilever**'s products are dealt with by the same team. Then when you say: 'is that Marmite?' the answer is 'yes'. But the answer is exactly the same if you say: 'is that Colman's Mustard, Lifebuoy soap, Domestos or Hellman's?'

The day I rang to ask why the label did not mention the place of manufacture my call was taken by a young Australian! 'You sound like you might prefer **Vegemite**,' I said. 'You're right, I do – I'm a traitor,' she laughed. She then went onto to tell me that she could

103

'guarantee' that Marmite is made in **Burton-on-Trent**. So why wasn't it stated on the label? 'It's not considered necessary information,' came the reply.

Unilever just don't make enough of what is a great PR concept. To start with you'd think they would give 'loveline', a capital promotional idea, a capital 'L' to go with it. But it's printed on the label without. And surely they could keep up the pretence of 'love' by at least answering with the name that matches the one on the label...

Finally, if you call outside working hours, a recorded message answers with: 'Marmite care line'. The message then gives special advice for anyone with a medical emergency. They're told to contact their doctor or NHS Direct, on 0845-4647. It's probably got more to do with Health and Safety than **allergies**. To be fair, it's not just Marmite because the message then advises callers with medical problems as a result of any other **Unilever** product to call 01-750-724746.

Lure: in a bizarre bid to lure ex-pat police officers back home from Australia, Leicestershire Police Force used Marmite as a way of reeling them in. The Homesick and Away advertising campaign was launched in December 2008, in the hope that the 130 vacancies on the force could be filled. It's reckoned that one in 11 of Australian police officers is British trained. Among the tempting 'come back' references used was Marmite, alongside real ale, roast beef, a British cuppa and Marks and Spencer underwear. So did the ploy work... or, did all the emigrating Bobbies fall for **Vegemite**? Leicestershire police spokesman Royston Brooks-Lewis revealed to me: 'We got 10 back.'

Lure-2: the British Tourist Authority has used Marmite in **advertising** and promotional material, to lure foreign visitors a couple of times. First, in 1997 it was featured among nine products considered iconic. The others were: NHS specs; Liquorice Allsorts; Vimto; Ben Sherman Shirts; the Mini car; Branston Pickle; Fisherman's Friend and Boddington's beer. The Marmite citation read: 'in its time (95 years and counting), Marmite has been credited with winning wars, preventing disease and most famously of all, providing that magic extra ingredient in British cuisine. Soups, sauces and stews, all would be lost without a blob of this darkly brown and gluggy extract of brewer's yeast. There the secret is out. It's seriously healthy of course, so much so that in the 1930s it was promoted with the catchy phrase: "It keeps nerves, brains and digestion in proper working order". No wonder Brits take a jar with them when they holiday abroad.'

Then 12 years on, BTA highlighted what it termed Classic British Kit to encourage visitors. This time the spotlight fell on people, genres and Marmite. It was the only icon, out of the original line-up, to survive. The new ones were: Aquascutum clothing; the jokes of Monty Python; Stephen Fry's wit; Morgan cars; burgeoning vineyards; Alexander McCall Smith's books and James Bond 007. This time the BTA – now operating under the Visit Britain slogan – said: 'Marmite still divides a nation and perplexes first-time breakfasters. Fans will insist its sharp, smooth flavour is unbeatable – and Marmite's century-old place in British larders suggests they've got a point.'

M

Marmalade: What does it have in common with Marmite? For one thing, regardless of how carefully you spread it without going close to the edge of the bread, it seems impossible to eat without getting your fingers sticky. Then see...

Marm-A-Lite: this is what double-M lovers have been waiting for. Marmalade and Marmite, together, in one jar. It's a merger meant to be: in the *Oxford Concise Dictionary* they could not be closer. They are listed one after the other. Of course, all anyone who wants to eat both together has to do is mix one with the other. But on that basis we would not have ready-made Yorkshire puddings, rice pudding in a tin, or sandwich shops. Artist Rex Aldred, he of the front cover design, also makes and sells a particularly fine marmalade. He obligingly put the theory to the test. The result? It's so good he's now making batches of Marm-A-Lite to order. But don't get too excited. If you want to buy some, you'll need to go to Whitby, North Yorkshire. Rex, who lives in a hamlet 10 miles out of the Yorkshire coast town, only sells locally in a couple of shops. But it's worth the trip, if not for the taste of his particular take on the M&M mix, but for the label! It claims: 'A Unique Experience For You & Your Toast', and goes on to say it's: 'Dark-Mysterious-Bitter-Sweet-Savoury'. Not quite as enticing as the wordage on his marmalade, which reads: 'Spread Some On Your Bits - Of Toast. Give Your Partner A Memorable Feast!' But there's no reason the same instructions shouldn't be applied to the Marm-A-Lite. Even Marmite haters might take to it. If not on toast then as a last minute 'slathering' onto barbequed sausages or grilled pork chops. It works superbly. To check on how to get your hands on this unique Marmite taste contact Rex via e-mail (see front of the book).

Marmalord: Steve Jones, of Croydon, will surely be a consumer of the above entry. His passion for marmalade is nudged at constantly by his desire for Marmite. The former is such that he's anointed himself, the Marmalord, which is the posh title that accompanies his 'job' as the curator of the World's First Museum of Marmalade. His virtual homage to the *other* quintessential British breakfast spread is contained on his website: *www.marmaland.com*. It's jammed with history, trivia, recipes - and understandable rants against **Unilever** for luring **Paddington Bear** away from marmalade into Marmite-land. Like many marmalade-aficionados he was not happy with the defection. 'Marmite put my nose out of joint a little by interfering with him.'

But Steve's distress at Marmite's owners failed to quell his appetite for marmalade and Marmite together. And the combo receives an honourable mention in his *A-Z of Marmalade*, appearing under Y for 'yeast'. Steve declares: 'Strangely, Marmite, the popular yeast extract which has been around since 1902, makes a happy bedfellow for marmalade. If you doubt me, try some marmalade and marmite sandwiches - 65/35 in favour of marmalade.' Steve is fond of eating his own words. His perfect start to a Sunday, he told me, is to breakfast on the two of them mixed together, preferably on toasted granary bread. 'I would describe myself as a fan of marmalade who flirts dangerously with Marmite,' he said.

marmite: but spelt with a lower-case initial letter and pronounced the French way, 'marmeet'. This makes it the traditional Gallic cooking pot, from which Marmite, many believe, takes its name. That assumption is based on the fact that the jar resembles the shape of the pot – narrow neck, bulbous body. A drawing of a 'marmeet' appears on the label. As it did on the original container. But that was not 'marmeet'-shaped. It was white earthenware and straight-sided. So, it's more likely the name came from 'petite marmite' - the basic French broth, made from vegetable stock, with pieces of meat added. And if the genesis of the name is rooted in petite-marmite, then it has to be pondered: who would ever have thought that Marmite was feminine!

Marmite: the Americans don't have Marmite but they do - or did - have marmites. That was the name of the US Army metal containers that took food into the field of battle. They are now highly collectable.

Marmite Prize: this has absolutely nothing to do with Marmite! The only thing the Marmite Prize shares with its namesake is a cult following. It's the art-child of London-based artists Marcus Cope and Stephanie Moran. They started it because of their boredom over most of the 'rated' prize exhibitions. 'They have become conservative, conformist - they have become predictable,' they wrote in the catalogue for the 2008 Marmite Prize. And the catalogue itself is very different. While 80 submissions were hung, all 300 entries (it costs only £10 to enter) were published in the catalogue. Other features set the Marmite Prize apart from the conventional. The first show, in 2006, saw the entries hung upside down! In 2008 they were displayed flush to the ceiling! It's also a nomadic show - always on the look out for avant-garde galleries. 'It helps our erratic display ideas if we are dealing with different spaces to hang the paintings,' Marcus told me. So what's with the name? 'It's a question we get asked all the time,' he said. 'And we always point out, as we do in our posters, flyers and website, we have nothing whatsoever to do with the yeast extract spread. Stephanie says we chose "marmite" to reclaim the word for marmites everywhere. I suppose, as artists, we felt the capitalists had stolen a word that belonged to a different tradition.' In honour of that philosophy, the first prize for the first show, was in fact a 'marmeet' cooking pot. In 2008 Marmite (with a capital M) was recognised. The winner was presented with a 500g jar of it, and the two runners up each went home clutching 250 g jars.

Marmite Sisters: again nothing to do with Marmite! Just another example of how the iconic product resonates. The Marmite Sisters were an indie band that, in the mid-80s, rocked the establishment. Well, the one around Leicestershire! The group, hailing from Glenfield - four miles from Leicester - is now sadly defunct. Mainly because the six guys in the band finally ended up getting 'proper' jobs. They were 'kids' when they started playing together. Graham Barnfield was the vocalist. Despite his youth (he was only 15) he had a powerful rocker's voice – when he wasn't drowned out by his mates, guitarists Steve Hill and Murray Coope, bass-player Christopher Murphy and Stub Robinson on drums. At first they called themselves, Anonymous. When they found out there was a band by that name in the States, they added an 'e'.

Then, when they all left school, they split for a

while but quickly reformed under another name, the Marmite Sisters. How did they come up with the name? You might imagine it was because they were all half-cut on strong lager, wolfing down a late night snack of Marmite sandwiches, while struggling to come up with a catchy name. But Graham, now a lecturer in journalism at the University of East London, told me it came out of a search for something with a fun, ironic twist – like a big time cabaret act from a small English town. That train of thought got all caught up with the bad dream Graham had of a dead mouse in a jar of Marmite. Not making a lot of sense? But then we are talking about a group of music-makers, influenced by punk, goths and progressive rock! The Marmite Sisters' first release was in 1988, with the *Kick Donkey* cassette followed a year later by the *Songs of Love and Lawnmowers*.

It was about this time that an order arrived for the two records from Best Foods Ltd, the then owners of Marmite. Steve - who is still known locally in Leicestershire and on various blog-websites, as Steve Marmite - told me: 'I sent the records off with a note saying that if they wanted us to change our name they could forget it, as Marmite is a cooking pot, etc, etc. They replied with a letter stating that "officially your band does not exist".' But it did – until the guys disbanded it in 1995, after recording *Gricers*, for a German label. It is still available, as other albums are, thanks to the internet. To hear the Marmite Sisters check out their site on *My Space*.

Memorabilia: there is nothing new about Marmite promotional items. Long before today's cake tins, lunch-boxes, coasters, egg cups, money boxes, thimbles, trays, memo-boards, pill-boxes, mugs and t-shirts, the various owners of Marmite flooded the market with special items. A personal favourite is the porcelain toast-rack, from the 1970s, which has a Marmite jar at each end. But the real collectibles are the special booklets put out by the Marmite Food Extract Company, the cooking books of yesteryear, the 'stamps' that were exchanged for gifts, old jars, original advertisements, the wooden boxes delivered to the grocer full of jars and the green and gold tins from the 1930s that the stock cubes came in.

Rare souvenirs from recent times are the sheets of I love/I hate stickers that were used during 1996 street polls to coincide with the cult **advertising** campaign. To determine how people felt, pollsters around the country asked people which camp they were in. Those who didn't know were offered a small square of bread with Marmite on. Their reaction was rewarded with an appropriate sticker. CPC, the owners of Marmite at the time, were clearly banking on the 'loves' winning the day. An A4 sheet of 70 stickers was by no means evenly divided: only 28 were stamped "I Hate".

Meridian: is a Marmite rival that comes in two varieties, one of which is 'no added salt'.

Both are fortified with a lot more B-12 (see **cyanocobalamin**) than Marmite: ie Marmite has only 15.0ug, compared to Meridian's 70ug. But Meridian has considerable less **Thiamin**, **Riboflavin**, **Niacin** and **Folic acid**. Unlike Marmite it lists B-6 (pyridoxine) as an ingredient, and the amount is elevated in the no-added-salt version, which could be good news for **PMS** sufferers.

Metal: Marmite has a lot of ingredients - including metals. Trace elements of cobalt and zinc, both of which are essential for good health, are found in it. Zinc is naturally in **yeast** and cobalt – no; it's not there to add a deep-blue colour – is a central component of B-12, which is added to Marmite.

Migraine: if you suffer from migraines you've probably worked out, or been told, that Marmite – indeed all **yeast** extracts – is a no-no. The charity, Migraine Action, names Marmite on its list of possible triggers. The culprit is tyramine, an amino acid found in fermented food. Which is why it occurs naturally in the lovely, black goo.

Milk-Shake: after cakes and Marm-A-Lite, why should a Marmite milkshake come as a surprise? The concept started with the Aussies and their **Vegemite**. For years they've boasted about shoving it into a milk-shake. That 'classic' recipe calls for beaten eggs, chocolate milk, bullion cubes, nutmeg. But the Brits don't like to mess around so much with their precious 'mite'. They have perfected a much simpler take on that magic way of pretending not to be eating ice-cream! The Shakeabout chain, with 10 outlets around the country, and more on the way, has made the Marmite-Milkshake a main feature of the dozens on offer.

Managing Director Rupert Verrell told me he originally insisted on Marmite being offered as a marketing tool. 'I thought it would be a good talking point. I had no idea it would take off like it has.' He tells a delightful story about opening day at the Eastbourne branch. 'An elderly man came in with three other people. He ordered the Marmite milkshake, and drank every drop. As he left I heard him say to his friends: "I can't believe I've waited 70 years to have that"!'

A huge dollop of the black goo is plonked into vanilla ice-cream and milk, given a good shaking and voila – 16oz of as creamy and salty a concoction as you could wish for. And all for £2.95. It seems that many who order a M-Milkshake do it as a dare... and fail to take more than a few sips. But there are many others who suck it up. Particularly at the Shakeabout in Liverpool's re-vamped downtown zone, on Paradise Street, where they sell more M-milkshakes than any other branch.

So, you don't live anywhere near a Shakeabout? You don't have to be deprived of this dubious treat. What are you waiting for? Grab some ice-cream, a hefty dollop of Marmite and get the blender out!

Moon, Rosemary: the well known TV cook and culinary demonstrator, was asked by CPC Ltd to write a Marmite cookery book. She revealed her response to the commission in the forward to the 1992 publication *My Mate Marmite In the Kitchen*: 'I really was a Marmite baby. I've always loved Marmite and was delighted to be asked to write this book. I hope you will enjoy trying the recipes as much as I've enjoyed creating them.'

Among the wide range of dishes, from soups and starters, to pizzas and pastas, main meals and sandwiches, Rosemary certainly created some very imaginative ideas. It's not every day you come across Aduki Bean and Date Casserole, where a hefty amount of Marmite is mixed with tomato puree and brown sugar, to create a sauce to complement a combination of beans, fennel, courgette, red pepper, onion and chopped dates.

She also included some nifty Marmite culinary tips. Like: blend Marmite into breadcrumbs to add a piquancy to coatings and toppings; save on cheese, in a cheese sauce, by adding Marmite, which will help maintain a strong flavour, despite using less of the main ingredient; give sausages a special twist by cooking them in the oven in a 50-50 mix of Marmite and water; give savoury pancakes a similar kick by adding Marmite to the batter; spread the bread cubes for croutons with Marmite; turn pumpkin and sunflower seeds into a totally tasty snack, by grilling them in a marinade of Marmite and water, until toasted.

The book was such a smash that Rosemary received a report of it being used by a chef in a hostel, high in the Himalayas. Today, she is still loyal to Marmite. So much so, that she told me: 'My last meal, if I have a choice, will be my husband's home-made bread, good butter, a generous smear of Marmite, strong Cheddar, lots of hot peppery watercress and mayonnaise. Hope I am not too ill to enjoy it!' (See also: **Cookery books**.)

Mosquitoes: for years there have been claims that Marmite offers excellent anti-mosquito protection. But is it an urban myth? Yes and no, depending on which report you read. Some data says, 'no way'. Other reports give it a thumbs up. Because of its high B-1 (**thiamin**) content many swear by consuming huge amounts of Marmite before venturing into mozzie-territory. The theory is that thiamin is excreted through the skin. While its odour cannot be detected by humans, mosquitoes do smell it. And they hate it.

... Now children Marmite a taste you will 'either love or hate...

116

Others say they've tried it, but to no effect. The belief that Marmite could ward off mosquitoes dates back to 1934, and the deadly malaria epidemic that hit Sri Lanka (then Ceylon). A British doctor, the late Mary Ratnam, started giving patients Marmite as well as the standard treatment of the day, quinine. The Marmite was reported to be more effective than the quinine. It appeared to revive the stricken and they were amazed how Marmite put some life back into them.

In April 2004 the belief was compounded when public health consultant Dr Martin Schweiger revealed to a conference in Leeds that Marmite did work. He told holiday-makers, heading for mosquito plagued regions, to pack plenty of Marmite. Confirming the Thiamin theory, he added: 'It's a simple trick that everyone can try.'

But four years later two malaria experts sounded the death knell for Marmite's anti-mosquitoes properties. In an article, published in the *British Medical Journal* in June 2008 David F Lalloo of the Liverpool School of Tropical Medicine, and David R Hill of the London School of Hygiene and Tropical Medicine, scotched the claims. In a list of 'popular' but 'ineffective' prevention practices, Marmite was right up there. Along with garlic, oil of citronella and electronic repellents.

In the end, maybe it's a case of mind over matter!

Museum: yes, there is a Marmite Museum.

And to continue the alliteration, it's in Missouri... in the USA. Now, what is America doing showing us the way home when it comes to collecting Marmite memorabilia? And it's not as if the 'curator' is a Marmite-mad ex-pat, surrounded by home-sick reminders and keepsakes. Doug Schneider is as American as they come.

He houses his big-M collection in the basement of his home, in Valley Park, a small town of 6,000 people, 20 Miles from St Louis.

Doug cultivated a taste for Marmite when he studied at the University of London, in the mid-70s, after serving in the Vietnam War. A friend introduced him to it. 'I found, once I learnt to apply it sparingly, that I liked the strong taste,' he says. These days he still eats it in a fairly conservative manner – on a buttered bagel – but it is his magic ingredient in the shrimp etouffee he specialises in. At last count Doug, who operates a billing service for the US freight industry, had upwards of 150 items in his collection.

His most prized possession is a rather lovely silver holder, with a handle and lid, which is inscribed 'Marmite'. But due to its cylindrical shape he feels it must be from Down Under. He knows it's commercially made, and not a piece of silverware bought privately, then inscribed, as he received a letter from Britain some years ago asking for help in identifying the same holder. And he feels it's not made by Sanitarium, the New Zealand makers of Marmite, in the same way the silver-lids in

Britain are not produced by Unilever.

Talking of lids, Doug wishes he'd kept that first jar he came across in London, the sight of which triggered a life-long interest in Marmite. 'I really liked the cute brown jar it came in. I should have kept that 1973 jar… It had a metal cap!'

Doug is happy to show off his 'museum' to visitors. To make a viewing date contact him by e-mail at: *ParadiseMO@aol.com*

Museum-2: Helen Graham does not have a museum - but she's getting close! She has a collection of 50 or so Marmite jars, plus an array of other Marmite products, like crisps, rice-cakes, crackers and some collectibles including the odd mug and recipe book. They cover three shelves at her home in Great Missenden, Buckinghamshire. She started her collection around 1970 when the round, bulbous shape of the jar, suddenly gave way to a straight-sided one. Shocked that the owners would do away with the familiar and traditional shape, she hung onto an old jar – and also kept the new one. Then when the old jar was brought back she kept that.

Since then Helen has kept an eye on the changing shape, and alterations made to the label and wording, always making sure an example of any change goes into her collection. Along with the special editions, like the **Champagne, Guinness** and the **cricket** ball, or promotional offers.

'We think nothing about the shape or label

has changed. But over the years it has. Quite subtle, but still changed,' she told me. Helen, apart from the straight-forward way of having it on toast and as a hot drink, likes to use Marmite in casseroles and stews. She also finds it's a good way of tempting her ageing dog to eat.

'It's quite pathetic, really, having a collection like this,' she laughs. 'But it isn't like I scour e-Bay for items. People do bring me things now.' One piece in her collection she likes to point out is the jar labelled Clinic Pack'. It was given out free to mothers at baby clinics, in the late 1970s. 'Of course there wasn't the awareness as there is today of how salt is a no-no. And we thought nothing of giving toddlers such a salty item.' Helen is not the only family with a 'thing' about Marmite. Her sister Victoria has a poetic take on it (see **Ode**).

N

Natex: the yeast extract that is preferred by many because of its extremely low salt content – just 0.4grams, opposed to Marmite's 3.9grams. But when it comes to B-12, which is added to yeast extracts (see **cyanocobalamin**), Marmite beats it, having much more of the vital vitamin. Also Natex does not list **Folic acid** or **thiamin** in its ingredients. Like so many of the Marmite alternatives, it has 'stolen' Marmite's colours. Its label is white, red and yellow; its plastic lid is yellow and it comes in a dark brown jar. It's made by **Jardox**.

Nature: in April 1933, the American edition of *Nature* announced, with obvious excitement, that it had received a booklet about 'something called Marmite'. It reported it had come from the Marmite Food Extract Company, in London. The scientific magazine, as esteemed then as it is now, reported that the booklet described the 'medicinal and dietetic value of this extract of **yeast**, rich in vitamins B. Its Vitamin B helps maintain the appetite and proper function of the digestive tract, and also aids growth, reproduction and lactation. The reserves in the body are very small, so that a regular daily intake is required.'

Netherlands: it's bad enough for fans to learn that Marmite was once owned by **Bovril**, and that both are now owned by the world's biggest producer of laundry soap, **Unilever**. But what isn't well known is that Marmite is now ultimately managed by the Anglo-Dutch conglomerate's Rotterdam operation. Though Unilever does go to pains to point out that Marmite's day-to-day activities still fall under the responsibility of its British office, in Leatherhead, Surrey, it downplays the 2008 Rotterdam move by saying it only reports into 'a business cluster' controlled in Holland. But in a way, whatever the management impact on the product, it is fitting. For Marmite has now gone full circle. Marmite's life began, in 1680, in Holland (see **Beginnings**). But because of the next entry, it is unlikely that Marmite will go the whole hog and follow that other great British dining-table icon, HP sauce - and end up being made in the land of dykes and windmills.

New: unless you are a regular reader of the *Food Trade Review* you're unlikely to know about the new Marmite plant, which started operating in 2008. The magazine, which provides technical information for those involved in the manufacturing and packaging of food, went into great minutia about the multi-million pound comprehensive upgrade of the factory, in **Burton-on-Trent**, that had seen few equipment changes in 50 years. Top of the 'must' list: improving production efficiency; lower maintenance; easier cleaning and energy savings. The major work revolved around redesigning the **yeast** extracting machinery - the pivotal part of the production-line. It underwent radical redevelopment. The biggest challenge there was to do it without compromising Marmite's distinctive flavour, appearance and gooiness (or viscosity, to give it its scientific name).

Unilever Project Manager Martin Beckford, told the magazine: 'Maintenance of the Marmite characteristics were so important, that while we were keen to make significant improvements in the plant, success or failure would eventually be judged on a product taste test.' With a startling array of high-performance, super-duper separators, nozzles, and filtration systems, production is non-stop, round the clock, round the year. It can handle 14 tonnes of water and autolysed yeast (that's when the salt has been added to break the yeast cells down) an hour. And it's designed to produce 5,000 tonnes of Marmite a year. To save you working it out, that's more than 10 million 500g jars. Sales can soar by many more millions, before Unilever has to think about expanding, as the new system has an in-built extra 30% capacity.

New-2: move over granola, there's a new breakfast bar on its way. No longer will you have to hang around at home to make the toast and get the dark brown jar out, just to eat that certain thing you cannot start the day without. Soon you will be able to rush off to work, school, or play, with a Marmite fix in your pocket, bag or briefcase. Marmite processed into a breakfast bar is being worked on by Unilever and it hopes to get it into the market-place some time in 2010. But be prepared for the quips. Like one Marmite fan, who on hearing about the Marmite Breakfast Bar, was so disappointed to hear it was going to be a processed snack – not a café in the high-street, offering, perhaps, a 'full English' to grapefruit segments or a freshly-baked croissant – all smeared with it!

New Zealand: Marmite is hugely popular with the Kiwis. As in Britain, it's part of the culture. Over the years, it has generated similar off-the-wall **advertising** and love/hate following. But while the name is the same - the product is different! (See **Sanitarium**).

Niacin: is one of the essential nutrients for humans. Better known as B3 and technically as nicotinic acid, Marmite packs plenty of it. In the old days when the horrible disease of **pellagra** was prevalent, it was also known as 'vitamin PP' (Prevent Pellagra) for its qualities in combating the condition. These days pellagra is rarely found in developed countries, as it breeds alongside poverty and malnutrition, but chronic alcoholism can trigger it. Also, communities that rely solely on a diet of maize (corn) are very susceptible, as it is the only grain that does not contain niacin. Meanwhile, for the population at large, niacin is very important in the treatment of high cholesterol. Exactly the opposite is the case for sufferers of gout; they should avoid anything containing high-levels of niacin.

Nipples: it is not unheard of for nursing mothers to dab Marmite on their nipples. There are two – very contradictory – reasons. Some do it to keep their tots happily on-the-tit; others do it to help wean their suckling babes. Either way it might explain why Brits, from birth, either love it or hate it!

Norwak, Mary: from an early age Mary Norwak's dual passion was writing and cooking. she combined the two into a hugely successful career as a cookery-writer. She worked for *Vogue* and *House and Garden*, and for 15 years was the cookery editor of *Farmers' Weekly*. Over the years she wrote about food for the *Daily Express, The Times* and the *Guardian* and has 90-plus cookery books to her name. At age 80 she had the joy of seeing her highly acclaimed *English Puddings* being republished, in July 2009. In 1981 her big-seller was the *Best of British Cooking*. She wrote it at the behest of **Bovril** Ltd, who owned Marmite. While there were recipes using Bovril cubes, and various Ambrosia products, like custard, rice-pudding and sago, which Bovril also owned, Marmite received main billing. But when I mentioned to Mary the Marmite recipes she had created, she roared with laughter. 'I absolutely hate Marmite,' she chortled. The Bovril link sold her on the idea, she recalled. 'I've always been a Bovril girl. When I was asked to do the book I think I just blocked out the Marmite bit. Though I did use it in a lot of the recipes.' (See also: **Cookery books).**

Nudity: what some will do to score, when it comes to pitching 'balls' in the yeast extract Ashes, the rivalry between Marmite and **Vegemite**... Phil Tufnell, former captain of the England cricket team stripped off to promote Marmite – while demeaning what he saw as the wimpy palates of the 2009 touring Australians. A Marmite marketing stunt saw a 15-metre high image of Tuffers in the buff being projected on to the side of the Aussie's London hotel, while playing the second test at Lord's. The strategically placed placard he was clutching was adorned with a giant picture of the special edition **cricket**-ball jar of Marmite emblazoned with the words: 'TOO TASTY FOR THE AUSSIES'. Not exactly a 'googly'!

O

Ode to Marmite: fancy getting lyrical about your favourite spread? Burst into prose with your thoughts (kind ones only, please) and you might see them used on the label. The back of a Marmite jar currently carries various poetic contributions from fans of all ages, accompanied by matching artwork.

A 250gram jar is adorned with: 'I don't think I'll ever write / a poem as lovely as Marmite.' It's apparently 'handwritten' on a piece of white bread and signed: 'By Matthew age 72'.

The 125gram jar has a drawing of a brown rose – to go with: 'Roses are red / violets are blue / you're brown / and I love you', and signed by 'Cheryl age 17½'.

On a 200gram squeezy jar, Lucy age 25, has come up with 'I like a good squeeze / between some bread & cheese!'

The Marmite-makers are looking for more poets to spread the word. Send your inspired words to:
marmite@unileverconsumerlink.co.uk

One example of a longer piece of poetry was penned by an ex-pat in a bid to explain the lure of it to Americans. It goes:

Marmite on toast or Marmite on bread,
Is a tasty British spread,
Filled with B vitamins, made from yeast,
Which is very healthy to say the least.
But Americans don't quite understand
The attraction that Brits have for this brand.
An acquired taste, a vegetarian treat
That young and old love to eat.
Marmite with honey or Marmite with jam,
Served as a sandwich on a slice of ham,
Sweet and savoury, deliciously flavoury,
There is nothing that compares just quite
To the taste of traditional British Marmite.

That is the work of Victoria R Crosby, who has lived in Glen Cove, a historic seaside town on the North Shore of Long Island, since the early 1960s. Apart from being a broadcaster and newspaper journalist, Victoria is a passionate member of the Daughters' of the British Empire, an organisation whose membership is made up of women who were born in Britain, or the Commonwealth, or can trace their ancestry to either. It has chapters all over the States and celebrated its centenary in 2009. Victoria penned her tribute to Marmite as part of a book of poetry she wrote in recognition of all things British. Other subjects she embraced poetically were the royal family and a cup of tea. Proceeds from PoeticVic-BritCentric, benefited the DBE and the British Memorial Garden, in Hanover Square, Manhattan, that has been created in memory of the British victims of 9/11.

For many DBE members Marmite is a memory of 'home' they hold dear, to such an extent that the website for the New Orleans chapter has a special section dedicated to it. Victoria, who grew up on the Wirral, is the only member of her household who touches it. Her husband and children have never got along with Marmite. But back home in Britain, Victoria's sister, Helen Graham (see **Museum-2**), is another devotee.

007: the current one, Daniel Craig, has Marmite to thank for getting him accepted into Equity, the actor's union. He qualified for his card – without which he would never have worked in the theatre or films – by starring in a TV commercial. As an unknown, dressed in a Marmite jumper, he assailed shoppers at a Reading supermarket, telling them how much he loved it. 'I was Mr Marmite,' he recalled. 'And that's how I got my Equity card.' In real life he loves Marmite. He's widely quoted as saying: 'I have it on my toast in the morning.

It wakes you up, like, "Welcome to the day! I've just put axle grease in my mouth".'

Organic: if the need for everything organic ruled your daily diet, Crazy Jack would have been the yeast extract spread for you. It was the only one that was organic. But it stopped being made in 2008. **Meridian** would be a natural to fill the gap, but as owner James Ashton told me: 'Due to the excessive cost of production, organic yeast extract has never been a commercial success in the UK, up to now.' Now the only organic yeast extract spread available in Britain is **Vitam-R**, which is made in **Germany**. But it is made from baker's, rather than brewer's, **yeast**.

Craig Sams and Jo Fairley, the dynamic organic duo who have given the world Green and Black chocolate - and are often hailed as running the greenest household in Britain - switched from Marmite to Crazy Jack several years ago. Until then Marmite was the only non-organic product in their Hastings home. They banished Marmite after a call from the Crazy Jack company. One taste of Crazy Jack and it was bye-bye Marmite! But they hung onto an empty Marmite jar – to kid the grand-kids. It used to be refilled with Marmite's usurper! The secret was revealed by American born Craig, the founder, along with his brother, of Whole Earth Foods. He told me: 'We put it in a Marmite jar to fool the grandchildren when they came over.' Now, with Crazy Jack having stopped trying to compete organically with Marmite, the Sams-

Fairley household has given up as well on having a yeast extract spread around. But then that doesn't bother Craig in the least. 'I don't eat the stuff!'

Outer Space: Marmite has been... everywhere! Even outer-space. The out-of-this-world trip was thanks to Yorkshire born NASA astronaut Dr Nicholas Patrick. He was on board the December 2006 shuttle flight. Each member of the crew is allowed a 'comfort food'. Dr Patrick, 45, took well... you-know-what. It had to be a squeezy – because they don't use knives in space.

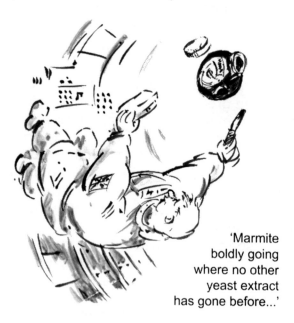

'Marmite boldly going where no other yeast extract has gone before...'

The Harrow and Cambridge educated Dr Patrick also had to make do with squeezing it on crackers. No bread in space either! It's too bulky and goes off quickly. What did his fellow astronauts say when they saw him squeezing black goo on a cracker and eating it? 'I'm not sure they noticed. You're so busy on these shuttle flights you don't have time to pay attention to such detail.'

Dr Patrick, is scheduled to go space-walking in February 2010. A squeezy will go with him. Until he talked to me, he had no idea that the squeezy version had been promoted with the introduction of Marmart (see **Art**). Remember he lives in Houston! It was suggested that, in the very unlikely event of him getting bored on his next trip into space he could use his comfort-food for a doodling session. After he stopped laughing at the thought, he explained: 'The way you do that on Earth is probably by holding the jar four inches or so over the toast and moving it around. But if you did that in space the Marmite wouldn't behave well. It wouldn't fall vertically. It would float in long strings all over the cabin and there'd be a big laundry problem!' So if, in early 2010, 'we have a problem Houston' is heard, we'll know Dr Patrick has been playing around with his comfort food...

Overworked: currently the most overworked metaphor in the British-English language is possibly: 'like Marmite'. It is used by people to describe themselves, particularly celebrities who consider themselves maverick; it's used by reviewers of films, books, the arts, exhibitions. It's virtually impossible to get through the day without hearing it, seeing it in print or hearing it broadcast. Its out-of-control usage – based on the 'love-hate' attitude towards Marmite that divides the nation – presents a challenge.

Overworked-2: but nowhere near as much as above... The use of Marmite in speech when trying to describe the impossibility of a task, as in: it's like making Marmite without a brewery. At least it's a twist on: couldn't organise a piss-up in one!

Own: it's easy to make your own... Or something similar. Use yeast flakes, available from most health food shops. Add a sprinkling of celery seeds and a blend of dried herbs and spices; a dash of soy sauce; a spot of old-fashioned gravy browning (just to add a richness of colour) and there you have it – a yeasty spread fit for any slice of toast!

I used Engevita, which is distributed in Britain by Marigold Health Foods, London. It's jam-packed with all the B-vitamins that Marmite is famous for, although it lacks B-12, which is added to Marmite. A primary strain of *saccharomyces cerevasiae*, the type of yeast that produces brewer's yeast, it is grown on enriched, purified molasses. It's produced in Holland, which adds another Dutch layer to the story of yeast extract. I will never, ever fall out with Marmite... but I have to confess I drooled over my own concoction.

Oxford: the Oxford Union debated Marmite in 1998. 'This House Hates Marmite' was the motion. Former MP and occasional TV personality Neil Hamilton led the charge challenging the motion. Which, as the *Independent* said: 'Shows he'll do anything for money.'

P

Paddington Bear: you'd have to be living in a Marmite mine not to know that the lovable Peruvian bear abandoned his staple diet of marmalade sandwiches and turned to Marmite ones – in the name of promoting the controversial squeezy container. But what you might have missed is that his creator, Michael Bond, was horrified at the switch. In September 2007 he wrote to *The Times* to express his displeasure and reveal he had not been consulted. By the time he found out what was going on it was too late. Paddington's characteristics are 'set in stone' he wrote. And his likeness for marmalade sandwiches are 'fundamental' to his being.

The twinning of Paddington and Marmite was agreed to by his daughter Karen Jankel, as managing director of Paddington and Company. As such, she has final approval on how PB – who arrived in Britain in 1958 – is used in merchandising. Karen had concerns about the merger, but she finally agreed, in exchange for a rather large but undisclosed amount of money, on the basis that she was sure Marmite would elevate Paddington Bear's image even higher than it already was. Which, frankly, it probably did.

Then, eight months into the row Michael Bond spoke out again. In an interview with the *Independent* in May 2008 he recalled his rage. 'I burst a lot of blood vessels, because it was done without my permission. I had an agency who looked after that side of Paddington. Normally they were left to their own devices and by the time I got to hear of it they had done some filming.' But Bond, who published *Paddington Here and Now*, the first novel about the bear in almost 30 years, around the same time, was relieved about one aspect of the controversy. 'I was able to change the script, the filming, in one way,' he disclosed. 'Paddington doesn't say, "I'm changing to Marmite".'

By March the next year, Paddington had turned his back on the interloper sandwich. The contract between the two iconic giants had ended and was not renewed. As Noam Buchalter, Marmite marketing manager, told the trade magazine *Brand Republic*: 'It was always intended that Paddington Bear was just trying Marmite in his sandwiches, for a change.' Maybe one day though he might get that Marmite yearning again, and so he doesn't do a repeat betrayal of marmalade, he could always try chomping on **Marm-A-Lite** sarnies!

Parliament: an early day motion in the House of Commons marked Marmite's centenary, in 2002, in lyrical terms. The late

Baron Stratford – aka Tony Banks, former sports minister, Labour MP for 22 years and vegetarian activist – invoked what he described as this 'wonderful savoury' as a subject worthy of debate. His motion read: 'We take intense satisfaction from the essential Britishness of the product and its lack of appeal for the majority of the world's population. And we look forward to another century of the wonderful savoury being spread over soldiers and crumpets.'

Parwill: It started as a **joke** for a name for the struggling rival product in Australia. 'Ma might, but Pa will' (get it?).

And for a time it was actually used as the name on the label. See **Vegemite** for the rest of the story.

Peace: Edward de Bono, the Maltese-born inventor of 'lateral thinking', wanted to use Marmite to bring peace to the Arab-Israeli conflict.

He wasn't suggesting bombarding the forever quarrelling leaders on the head with jars of it, but force-feeding it to them. His theory: as eaters of unleavened bread, they were not consuming enough zinc. The mineral, which is found naturally in **yeast**, is essential for the maintenance of high-levels of tolerance and low-levels of belligerence. He actually suggested his Marmite Peace Plan to the Foreign Office, in 1999. His bone-headed idea sank like a sack full of giant jars of Marmite chucked into the Red Sea.

But de Bono, author of 62 books translated into 37 languages, will never be allowed to forget it. He's teased and ridiculed on the internet, particularly on *Uncyclopedia*, the spoof version of *Wikipedia*. On a writing site spawned out of the BBC shutting down its 'Get Writing' department, aspiring writer Jane Powers, from Nottingham, nailed de Bono's non-starter peace-project, in a very funny Marmite satire. Jane led off by reporting that Tony Blair was in favour of the Marmite peace-plan. 'Cherie always puts it on my soldiers, it keeps me calm,' she had him saying. 'I'm trying to persuade Prescott to try it before he twats someone again.' Reaction from the Middle East was mixed, she said. Hamas denounced it as an evil Zionist plot to de-lead the pencils of Arab men; while a Fatah spokesman admitted that, while he thought Marmite had its place in the world, he only used it to keep the camels off his dates. As for the Knesset, all a spokesman would say was: 'Sweet Jesus, you guys actually eat this?' Dr de Bono declined to comment. But Jane told me: 'I did think de Bono's idea one of the more outlandish solutions to the Middle East.' To read her full satirical take on it, go to: *www.greatwriting.co.uk*

Pellagra: is a particularly nasty wasting disease, both gastrointestinal and neurological, that inevitable ends in death. Caused by a **niacin** deficiency, it is characterized by dermatitis, diarrhoea and dementia. Generations ago it reached epidemic proportions in the American South, because of a diet reliant on maize, the only grain that does not contain niacin. The United Nations International School, in New York, has underlined how useful Marmite is in treating the horrible condition. Pupils doing Higher Level Biology, studying Pellagra in the second term, are told that a way to ensure a sufficient niacin intake is to eat Marmite. The course paper states: 'Marmite is a rich source of niacin - and delicious!

Petite: sadly the inconceivable has happened. The petite jars of Marmite – the teeny 57gram – have disappeared, banished from the production belt in 2006. There was always enough in there to make an ample tureen of petite marmite, the traditional French broth. And for travelling, they were perfect. Even more so today, with the airline hand-baggage travel restrictions.

Now the smallest jar available is 125grams.

Philby, Kim: even spies sometimes need to turn to conventional means to get their hands on something they desperately need. Like Marmite. When double-agent, Kim Philby – the infamous 'Third Man' – defected to Russia, in 1963, he was treated like royalty. The best of everything was lavished on him. Even so, his VIP life in Moscow lacked one thing: Marmite. When his son John visited him for the first time, Philby confessed his longing. After that John always arrived in Moscow laden down with jars of Marmite. Happily for his dad, who died aged 76 in 1988, John made the trip at least a dozen times.

Pickle: nothing to do with mixing Marmite into piccalilli (though that's an idea to explore). But all to do with Pickle the pet cockerel who was suffering from a crippling disease. In June 2008 Pickle – according to the *Daily Mirror* – had a tough time strutting around his pen in Reepham, Norfolk. His frantic owner, Sarah Oates, called in the vet who quickly diagnosed that the scrawny nine-week old rooster had a B1 vitamin deficiency. The tell-tale sign was the way his claws had curled-up, making it impossible for Pickle to get around. 'Give him Marmite,' the vet ordered. Sarah did, by smearing it on his beak and Pickle licked it off, placing himself firmly in the 'love' camp –and on the road to recovery.

Pigs: young pigs are prone to a distressing

condition, colloquially known as Marmite Disease. Its proper name is *exudative epidermitis*. As it suggests, it causes them to ooze fluids, which are dark in colour and greasy in texture. According to *Saunders Comprehensive Veterinary Dictionary* affected pigs look as if they have been smeared in Marmite. The disease is usually a result of injury or inflammation.

Plants: empty Marmite jars do have a great use. A really good one is to start seedlings. The darkness of the glass will protect the roots – which do not do well exposed to light – and the jars certainly look a lot nicer than those black plastic boxes.

PMS: you will often read that Marmite is a 'cure' for pre-menstrual syndrome. It's the B-6 (pyridoxine) that naturally occurs in yeast extract that supports the theory, because it can help reduce the bloated feeling that is a major PMS symptom. But the amount of B-6 is so little it's not even listed on the label and you'd need to consume a 125gram jar a day to get enough to have any chance of beating the bloating. But it would be a bid that would be totally defeated by the simultaneous high salt intake, which would work against the B-6, with its well known water-retention properties. **Meridian**, a Marmite alternative might provide a better chance of some relief.

Poll: in a poll taken in 2007 by the BBC food magazine *Olive*, Marmite came both top and bottom! Readers voted it the best British food, at the same time as saying it was the worst. It topped fish and chips and Yorkshire pudding. But tripe and black pudding was favoured over Marmite by others.

Poll-2: in 2008, an internet firm polled 5,000 people as to their love or hate for Marmite. By the narrowest of margins — 53% — the 'love' lot came top. And the widest spread of fans, the *Daily Mirror* reported, was in the North, with a big concentration of them in Sheffield, Manchester and Newcastle. For some inexplicable reason the survey revealed that it was least popular in Brighton and Coventry.

Poo: in a hysterically funny book about human faeces, *What's Your Poo Telling You?* Marmite gets a mention... On page 83 authors Dr Anish Sheth, a gastroenterology Fellow at Yale University, and Josh Richman, talk about a new-born's first bowel-movement as resembling Marmite. The technical name for this pediatric poo is 'meconium' and they write: '...it shares its green-black colour and pasty texture with Marmite, the pungent yeast-base spread of the Brits, and **Vegemite**, beloved by the Aussies, but thankfully lacks their overpowering aroma.' Since the book's 2007 publication, the analogy has gone into popular use for when baby-poo comes up. Or out! Among the many references is the one on *ukfamily.co.uk* (a website that's part of the Walt Disney company). When talking about baby's first bowel-movement it states: '...it looks like a cross between tar and Marmite.'

Popcorn: for an in-heaven taste, add Marmite to melted butter and pour over freshly-popped popcorn!

POWs: Marmite was a life-saver for many. It was a mainstay item in humanitarian food-packs the Red Cross sent to POWs of both WWI and WWII. The B-vitamin richness kept many a starving prisoner alive. Particularly those held captive by the Japanese, in the Second World War. Beriberi was a common killer condition – that also rendered sufferers blind – because of the polished rice diet they were forced to exist on. Polishing rice removes the outer layer that contains **thiamin**, commonly referred to as B1. Also, the general lack of vitamins generally resulted in a horrendous condition, particularly prevalent among those held at the notorious Changi Camp in Singapore. A swelling and rawness of the testicles, it was officially called diphtheria scrotum. But the men predictably nicknamed it Changi Balls.

The late artist Leo Rawlings, one of the lucky survivors – whose sketches and drawings from those dark days are famous – wrote a book of his horror-experiences, *And the Day Came Like Thunder.* An extract is reprinted on the *FEPOW* (Far East Prisoners of War) website. In it he relates how a prisoner, who was working outside the camp, managed to get his hands on some Marmite. Knowing it contained vitamins that might cure, or at least relieve, Changi Balls, he handed it over to the hospital. It was given to a patient who was told to use it up as soon as possible. A couple of days later he was asked if it had helped. 'He thought it had,' Rawlings wrote. 'But, by gum, it had smarted when he put it on!' This might well be an apocryphal yarn. But it also emphasises the healing qualities of Marmite.

On a more sombre note, from those days, another POW tells how supplies of Marmite would have saved so many of his fellow-prisoners. On a similar website – *COFEPOW* (Children of the Far East Prisoners of War) – Bill Anderson, who served in the 9th Battalion, the Northumberland Fusiliers, reveals how the Red Cross parcels did not reach everybody. He posted an account about the horror and medical trauma of getting beriberi, dysentery and cholera. He lived, as many around him died. When he returned home to Gateshead he weighed six stone. He finished his emotive story with this conclusion: 'You don't need a lot of food. You want stuff with vitamins. Actually if we'd had Marmite, nobody would have died at all. It's got about all you need in it.'

Promite: another Marmite imitator; another Australian yeast extract. It's been around since the 1950s and differs from its main rival **Vegemite**, not to mention Marmite, in that it contains sugar. Also in the mix is starch thickener, lactose, caramel colouring and vegetable gum. It was originally made by the Australian food company Henry Lewis, under the Masterfood brand, before it was taken over by the giant Mars family group in 1967.

Pronunciation: there was a time when, apparently, it was common-pace for Marmite the product to be pronounced the French way, 'marmeet'. There was a fun reminder of this in a letter to the ***Independent***, which was part of the avalanche of correspondence revolving around Marmite in 2006. Colin Murison Small wrote: 'So far your cache of Marmite folklore has not raised the question of the correct pronunciation of the word. Today's Marmite **advertising** suggests it rhymes with "might", not "meet". However, during a heated argument in about 1937 a friend telephoned the firm and asked: "Is that the Marmite factory?" Only to be put down by the receptionist with her tart reply: "Marmeet, madam".'

Colin, the entrepreneur travel expert, who invented 'chalet-party ski-ing' in 1958 and now specialises in 'Hidden Greece', told me: 'Up until the war I remember "marmeet" was the way the company liked it pronounced. Actually it was my parents who were arguing over the way to say it. And my mother rang the factory to settle it. But then Marmite changed it when they wanted to make rhyming advertising slogans and jingles.'

His theory was backed by a subsequent letter to the *Independent*, that had been prompted by his. Jacqueline Woodfill, of Iffley, near Oxford, wrote to point out: 'A clue to the pronunciation of Marmite lies in an advertisement from my childhood, that went something like this:

If Ma might give me Marmite for my breakfast.
If Ma might give me Marmite for my tea.
If Ma might give me Marmite for my supper.
How happy I and Pa and Ma might be.

Mrs Woodfill, 87, told me: 'The change must have been a little earlier than the late 1930s. I was a child when, because it was so funny, my father used to read the rhyming advertisement to me out of *The Times*.'

Prostitute: in old Parisian patois, slang, 'marmite' was the term for a whore.

Publications: whichever company has owned Marmite over the years it has published books. Mainly **cookery** books. But there have been a few non-food publications, mainly in the 1930s, by the original owners, the Marmite Food Extract Company. One was an eight page booklet called *Safety First*. Using colourful, comic-strip illustrations, it gave instructions to children on how to cross the road and ride a bike. And in 1937 the company brought out the *Coronation Souvenir*, to mark the ascent of King George VI to the throne. And now, for the true, no holds-barred, lovers of the spread, we have the *Bumper Book of Marmite*. Published by Absolute Press, the company that published Paul Hartley's cookery book it is sanctioned by **Unilever**, the current owners of Marmite. It explores the 'strange, beautiful, funny world of Marmite... with glorious menu ideas and jolly clever ideas for jar-scraping...'

Q

"What now! Squeezy Marmite?"
"Philip, one's royal family must attempt to keep up
with the times."

Queen: from 1987 until 2007, Sir Robin Janvrin was a senior Buckingham Palace aide. For his last eight years he was the Queen's Private Secretary. Shortly before his retirement, according *The Grocer*, he compared the Royal Family to Marmite, saying that it had moved with the times. And added: 'the changes have been made gradually and with respect for tradition'.

Quirky: It's mentioned frequently, particularly in the **Unilever** sanctioned *The Marmite Cookbook*, that the British Olympic team, for the Melbourne Games of 1956, was sponsored by Marmite. Yet the British Olympic Association has no record of it!

Quirky-2: how in 2006, the US site of *amazon.com* had a deal that combined an Apple-Mac product with Marmite. Buyers of the computer company's $108 4.0 online service were rewarded with a 12-pot pack of Marmite.

Quorn: is a perfect match for Marmite. A hefty dollop of Marmite in pasty looking, tasteless, Quorn is a quick and easy way of turning this base of many a vegetarian dish into a palatable one. Surprisingly they have something in common: brewer's yeast, the starter for Marmite, and mycoprotein, from which Quorn is derived, are both fungi. And Quorn certainly smells a bit yeasty.

Quote: '...the world is divided into those who like Marmite and those who are imbeciles...' anon – although thousands out there will surely claim authorship!

Quote-2: '...the government gets through home secretaries like most families get through jars of Marmite: each lasts a little over a year...' Simon Hoggart, political commentator in the *Guardian*, 26 June, 2009.

R

Rations: when the soldier guys and gals fighting in Afghanistan and Iraq delve into their emergency ration packs, what a disappointment they face. No Marmite! Ok, so it's not there. Why should it be? Half the population can't stand the stuff. Point taken. But then not everyone, by a long chalk, is a hot-sauce fan. And yet there's a tiny bottle of Tabasco in there – which can be added to the packet of Thai green curry, if it isn't spicy enough.

In May 2009, the Ministry of Defence introduced this over-hauled 24 Hour Multi-Climate Operational Ration Pack. Considering the part Marmite has played in keeping British **POWs** alive through two world wars it's a shock to discover a sachet is not tucked away among the Typhoo tea-bags and Shrewsbury biscuits. And after soldiers serving in Kosovo wrote to the Marmite factory, begging for emergency supplies in 1999, you'd have thought it would always have been on hand for those on the front-line. But in the end it was the rank and file themselves that gave

Marmite the thumbs-down. An MoD spokesperson told me: 'It does not feature in the new MCR as a result of food selection panels which are carried out with a range of military personnel. The panels determined that it wasn't something they wanted.'

But when it comes to the general purpose Operational Ration Pack the contents are a bit different. There is a yeast extract item included. But it's not Marmite! The MoD initially called it 'a similar product'. So what is the name of it? 'It's not a recognised brand,' was the official answer. Which does not sound right, as the manufacture of yeast extract spread is not something that is just churned out at will. It's the result of an extremely complex formula and process. Under pressure to clarify, the MoD explained: 'Under EU regulations we're not allowed to name it.' But then a little birdie revealed the shameful 'secret'. It's **Vegemite**! Clearly the inclusion, of the great opposition to Britain's national food treasure, is down to all those Aussie's who serve in HM forces!

Real Marmite: the summer of 2009 saw intriguing wordage being used on the official Marmite website. On the shopping page, in among the I love/I hate t-shirts, cake tins and other kitchenware, there was a come-on to buy the spread. 'New Real Marmite Now in Store!' it announced. What did it mean? The 'real' bit? This was the 'real' Marmite as opposed to what - the imitation, the bogus, or **Vegemite**? Of course none of the three products offered for sale – a special edition **cricket** jar, a squeezy or a regular 250gram jar – was 'new'... So 'real' Marmite...? A call to the 'Marmite **loveline**' didn't provide an answer. The poor chap who took the call tried to help but of course he couldn't, because there was no answer: apart from it being the work of a copy-writer who knew not of what he or she wrote!

Reformite: this could have, should have, been the first Marmite. It's the Dutch version of Marmite. Or, was. And on the basis it was in 1680 a Dutch scientist (see **Beginnings**) who detected that brewer's yeast-sludge had potential as something other than a 'chuck-away' mess, it could have beaten Marmite into the market-place by centuries. But, like all the other yeast extract spreads, it wasn't 'invented' until Marmite had shown the way. It was sold only in health food shops – hence the name 'reform' which in Dutch refers to 'reform huis', which translates to health food shop – and disappeared in the early 1950s. It gets an honourable mention in a collection of war-time diaries and letters, written by a young Jewish woman, Etty Hillesum. They cover the darkest days of the German occupation, from 1941 until her death in 1943, at age 29. In one letter she writes: '....do you know a product called Reformite? It's something like Marmite and you spread it on bread. It has helped to keep mother's appetite up...' Etty's writings were published in book form in 1981. Information on the history and fate of Reformite is sparse. An internet search found mention of it in a fragment of a letter, dated 1944. The writer is asking a friend to visit and to bring with him a newspaper and some Reformite.

Remote: the most remote display of Marmite is in Antarctica. But as welcoming a sight as it is to see jars of it so far from home, there's not a smear of it to be had. For the kitchen that it is in is part of the remotest museum in the world. It's in Port Lockroy, a natural harbour in the British Antarctic Territory, which was discovered by the French in 1903. But the British quickly took it over, first using it as a whaling station, then as an operations base during World War II, before it became a research station. It was abandoned in 1962. Everything was just left. Including the grocery supplies. And when, 30 years later, it was decided to save it as a museum rather than demolish it, the cans and jars of food were left intact. Which is why we know Marmite was an essential part of the rations the polar explorers took with them.

The amount of Marmite and packets of Marmite cubes is eye-catching. The museum is one of the most popular destinations for the burgeoning tourism trade to Antarctica. Operated by the United Kingdom Antarctic Heritage Trust, Port Lockroy is looked after for the four 'summer' months of the year it welcomes visitors by Rick Atkinson and a couple of helpers. And no, they never feel like raiding the Marmite pantry. Not because they can't stand it – but they take enough with them to last the long tour of duty.

...Although the visitors often lust after it, like Geordie David Lees whose eyes popped when he made it to Port Lockroy, when he was travelling the world with his now wife, Emma. She blogged about their adventures and after landing at Port Lockroy wrote: '...after more penguin watching we go inside and see the living quarters of previous expeditions. The main thing that hits us is the quantity of Marmite. Dave is jealous...' Dave, who is now living in Brisbane with Emma and their young son, has tried all the antipodean versions but still maintains his love of Marmite. But he's bringing his son up on **Vegemite**. His supply of 'real' Marmite is too precious to allow anyone else a taste! 'Cruel I know,' he told me. 'But he is an Australian, so he might as well grow up with his heritage.'

Rhyming-Slang: Marmite is in the lexicon of Cockney rhyming slang. As in: 'talking a load of Marmite...'

Riboflavin: which is found in abundance in yeast extract, is a key reason why Marmite, and all the imitators, comes in dark glass jars. Exposure to light destroys it. Better known as B-2, it is essential for good health. It's important in the production of red-blood cells and aiding carbohydrates to release energy. The body doesn't store riboflavin, so daily intake is necessary. Happily it is found naturally in many foods, with prime sources other than yeast extract being eggs, dairy products, green leafy vegetables, nuts and liver. A good broad diet ensures a plentiful intake, therefore a deficiency is rare. But key symptoms pin-pointing a lack of it are cracked lips, scaly skin, anaemia and sore throats. An extra intake of Riboflavin is also now recommended in the treatment of migraines. But **migraine** suffering Marmite-lovers should not dive into the jar and gobble it down by the spoonful. In fact they should do the exact opposite – and not touch it, at all. Tyramine, also found naturally in yeast extract, can induce migraines.

Royal: the Marmite label does not display the 'By Royal Appointment' seal. And if it was entitled to, then surely it would. Goodness knows why it isn't. Enough Marmite certainly seems to be eaten behind royal walls – and on shooting picnics – to warrant a warrant. The Queen and, by all accounts, most of the Royal Family, are Marmite lovers (although simply by the law of averages there's got to be some of them that hate it...) and it's always on hand in HM's pantry. This according to Nottingham-shire born Darren McGrady, who went to cook at the Palace in 1982. He stayed for 11 years, before becoming personal chef to Princess Diana for the five years before her death in 1997.

Asked about the Marmite habits within the Palace he revealed: 'Marmite was very popular at Buckingham Palace, especially at tea-time.' Straight-forward Marmite sandwiches were the order of the day. But for a little extra flourish, 'a piece of butter lettuce' was added. At Balmoral the chosen way was for it to be 'brushed lightly' on crumpets.

Darren – who has now carved out a celebrity cooking career in America – also used to regularly serve Gaelic Steaks. But with a twist. He would add a dollop of Marmite to the traditional heavy cream-whisky sauce. And the one who loved it most? 'It was a hands-down favourite of the Duke of Edinburgh,' reveals Darren. 'If he'd had his way, it would have been on the menu every day.'

The recipe is featured in his 2007 book: *Eating Royally – Recipes and Remembrances from a Palace Kitchen*. But it can be easily accessed by going to Darren's website: *www.theroyalchef.com* and clicking on the February 2008 newsletter.

S

Salt: there's too much for some, in Marmite. Of course, for true fans, that's why they love it. In 2007 **Unilever**, aware of the need for people to cut-back on salt-overload in the interest of good health, reduced it from 4.3grams per 100grams, to 3.9grams. The whole business of salt intake is confused by the reference to sodium. The important thing to remember is that all salt is sodium, but not all sodium is salt, which is why the Marmite label also lists: 'Salt (based on sodium)'. The Marmite '**loveline**', which gets lots of calls about the confusion, explains it easily: to get the 'salt' content, multiply the sodium by 2.5. For Marmite this comes in at 9.75grams although the label, just to be on the safe side, rounds it up to 9.8grams.

Unlike most other yeast extracts, Marmite does not offer a 'reduced salt' or 'no-added-salt' version. A good example of the difference between sodium and salt comes from Meridan, which is made in Sutton Scotney, Hampshire, and is available in health food shops. It produces what it calls 'natural' yeast extract, which contains a whopping 5grams of sodium, per 100grams. In sharp contrast, its 'no-salt-added' version has barely a trace at 0.3grams. **Natex**, also available in health food shops, is 'salt-reduced', which in its case is 0.4grams – only slightly more than 'no salt added'. The German made **Vitam-R**, which sells in Britain under the Essential label, has 1.6grams of sodium. While **Vegemite** –which like Marmite has just one version - has 3.5grams which when translated to 'equivalent as salt' is 8.5grams. At least that's what the label states. Unlike Marmite, the Aussie lot round the figure down! It is, in fact, 8.75grams.

But just to get the whole salt thing into perspective, Marmite is by no means an offender when it's compared to its stable-mate **Bovril**. Its sodium content is a beefy

4.51grams per 100grams, which means its salt is 11.50grams.

Sandwich: American rock band Roots, the house-band for the top-rated Jimmy Fallon late-night TV show, has code phrases for each piece of music they play. In February 2009 drummer Ahmir 'Questlove' Thompson discussed the musical interludes that typically break-up all the US late-night shows, with *Rolling Stone* magazine. He said that while they're traditionally dubbed 'beds' or 'bumpers' in the industry, he calls them 'sandwiches'. As he explained: '...when we're referencing some UK rock shit, that's the Marmite sandwich. If it has a didgeridoo, then it's a Vegemite sandwich.'

Sandwich-2: in June, 2009, the *Daily Mirror* ran the Great British Sandwich contest. It was in response to a poll rating cheese as the number one filling. Boring, said the *Mirror*. Its readers responded by the hundreds, when the paper asked for 'more inspired' suggestions. Appropriately Lord John Edward Hollister Montagu, the 11th Earl of Sandwich, whose ancestor invented the snack of something between two slices, judged the contest. And yes, Marmite was an ingredient in the top ten line-up. Paul Murphy of Bristol paired it with chips, smashed between buttered, crusty white bread. But the good Lord did not take to it. After one bite he'd had enough. His comment: 'Marmite has its place, but I'm not sure this is it.'

Sanitarium: this all sounds very clinical. But

then it is, because this is the North American spelling for 'sanatorium', which still doesn't throw any obvious light on why it's an entry. Especially when you learn that it's about New Zealand, which only compounds the oddity. It's all to do with the manufacture of Marmite in New Zealand. And even then it's not 'real' Marmite (as you will see as you read on). Sanitarium is the name of the company that makes it. So what on earth has a place for the convalescing got to do with Marmite? Well, nothing. It's just the trading name chosen by the Seventh Day Adventists who make the so-called Marmite in New Zealand.

In 1900 a leading member of the American headquartered church went Down Under after training at the famous Michigan Battle Creek Sanitarium, which pioneered the healthy lifestyle movement and was operated by the Church. He started a 'sanitarium' in Christchurch. One of the first products the company became involved with was Marmite. It was imported directly from Britain and the Kiwis quickly fell in love with it. Then the outbreak of World War I interrupted supplies and Sanitarium, realising what a great product they were missing, very cleverly started negotiating with Marmite in a bid to get its hands on the 'secret' formula and the right to use the name. In 1919 The Marmite Food Extract Company agreed, granting the Sanitarium Health Food Company exclusive rights for both manufacture and distribution throughout Australasia.

The only 'right' they didn't acquire was the shape of the jar.

Over the years Sanitarium have messed with the ingredients, until today its Marmite tastes very different from the 'proper' Marmite. The high sugar content is to blame. And the sweetness is palatable. And all this to tell you that the New Zealand made yeast extract is the only one in the world called Marmite that is not Marmite! As for the 'real' Marmite - because the original owners parted with the rights - that cannot be sold under its original name in either New Zealand or Australia. There it's called 'Our Mate'.

Sausages: what a lucky lot the Marmite lovers in the Buckinghamshire town of Hazlemere are... They have their very own Marmite treat: Marmite sausages, made by the famed butchers in town, Hall's of Hazlemere. Of the 20 different types of sausage Halls make each day, the M-sausage – pork, thick and £8.99 a kilo - is an absolute top-seller. They've been a mainstay of Hall's fine offerings since 1999. Then in 2004 they beat 112 other entries to win the Gold Medal at the prestigious Smithfield Sausage Awards. Owner Graham Hall told me: 'With Marmite and top quality pork as the ingredients they were always going to be a winner. And their popularity continues to grow. They fly off the shelves and it looks like we'll be making them for years to come.'

Shoe-polish: Japanese **POWs**, lucky enough

to get Red Cross rations, had a great ruse that allowed them to hang onto the Marmite that was part of the emergency parcels. The Japanese guards were always very keen to help themselves to any goodies. But the prisoners, desperate not to lose the goodness of vitamin-fortified Marmite, would often tell them it was boot-polish! Even going to the extent of sacrificing a dab or two to demonstrate how good it was for that job. Many years later the *Wall Street Journal* – in a feature on the aforementioned Myers of **Keswick** – described the shop's huge seller as 'flavoured shoe polish'!

Slugs: and snails love Marmite. So much so their desire for it will kill them – or drown them, actually. Insert bowls full of diluted Marmite (watered down with beer works well, as they're partial to that too) into the ground and watch the slugs and snails that have been plaguing your garden or allotment, race towards them – then plunge in and be unable to crawl out.

Not very nice. All a bit cruel, perhaps, but better for gardeners than watching them destroying their plants.

Song: penned by folk-guru Kevin McGrath the *Marmite Song* is hysterical. The refrain goes: 'the **Bovril**'s with the gravy but the Marmite's with the jam'. What sort of nonsense rhyme is that? Well, it's worth remembering when you're searching for your favourite yeast extract spread in Tesco, or most of the other supermarkets. Unless you are familiar with the one you're shopping in, you will not find Marmite easily. Kevin wrote the *Marmite Song* in 1994 after visiting a new Tesco in his home town of Harlow, Essex.

He had a huge problem finding Marmite. Horrors, had it been banished in favour of Tesco's own? No, there was no sign of the imitator either. Finally a store assistant came to Kevin's rescue. She directed him away from the section with condiments like ketchup, mustard, gravies and all things savoury and led him to the section containing marmalades, honey... and jam.

Now, you understand the refrain. After that cock-eyed experience, Kevin went home and penned the song. To this day it is still the one, out of his wide repertoire of folk-songs, he cannot get away without singing. Kevin, a retired social-worker, tells me: 'I've written a few hundred songs. But the *Marmite Song* is the one that works best with listeners. I wish I could work out why it's funny. Of all the songs I've written this is the one that hits the spot. I like to think it's the underlying theodicy of the text.' And famed singers have helped spread the popularity of the song. The late Irish balladeer Frank Harte often entertained audiences with it. And Scottish folk-artist star Adam McNaughtan has added to its popularity.

The first verse goes:

'I was so lost in Tesco's, in an endless maze of shelves,
  Where those trolley pushers jostled, being each one for themselves.
  I was hunting for the Marmite, which was nowhere to be found,
  And I'd searched through rows of pickles,
  As I wandered round and round.
  Then a wandering assistant came to help me as I cried,
  And I reached out with a trembling hand, and asked – and she replied,
  'Oh the system's very simple, if you understand the plan,
  The Bovril's with the gravy, but the Marmite's with the jam'.

To be fair to Tesco, it's not alone in its locating of Marmite. Many of the other supermarkets put it with the jams, well away from the Bovril. A Tesco spokesman explained: 'The vast majority of customers put Marmite on their toast or in sandwiches. Therefore that is why it is found alongside other products that customers use in a similar way.' To sing along through the other two verses of Kevin's song go to: *www.mudcat.org*

Song-2: penned to rile the visiting Australian **cricket** team during the fight for the 2009 Ashes. It was sung by Tuffers and the Wooden Urns, aka former England bowler Phil Tufnell and a crowd of his cronies, to cheer on England captain Andrew Strauss and 'our boys', to smack it to the Aussies. Sponsored by Marmite, the song sneered at the Australian team for their addiction to **Vegemite**. In the video, Phil sported a Marmite t-shirt as he and his cricket choir belted out: 'Put Marmite on your sarnie, that other stuff is wrong. We are Andy's army and this is our Ashes song!' The video could be downloaded for 79p a time to raise money for the Cricket-for-Change charity, of which Phil is president. Or, for those too tight to part with that piddling amount, it could be seen and heard on *Facebook*.

Launching the song, Phil said: 'Having been sledged by the Aussies many, many times myself, I am delighted that Marmite has enabled me to finally get my revenge with this belter of a tune, while also being able to show my love for the England team and support Cricket for Change, which is very close to my heart.' But a rather odd aspect of the Marmite v Vegemite musical fun-and-games is that it was sung to the tune of that well known Australian song, Two Little Boys, penned and sung by that enormously Australian character Rolf Harris. Go figure!

Spurgeon: in Victorian days, Charles Haddon Spurgeon was known as the 'Prince of Preachers'. He still is, to his vast global following. This man of Essex, who achieved fame on a world pulpit, was a Reformed Baptist minister (b. 1834, d.1892). It's said he 'spread the word' to more than 10 million people, as he preached – at the peak of his popularity – sermons at the rate of 10 a week. What in heaven's name has all this to do with Marmite? It's not as if he was an avowed fan; he couldn't have been: he died before it was invented. But one of his greatest followers is an American pastor, Phil Johnson, of Sun Valley, California, who hosts a website devoted to everything Spurgeon. Which really makes the Marmite connection even murkier... But enter Marmite into any search-engine and up comes *The Marmite FAQ* under the website *spurgeon.org.* It runs for 15 pages, and is extremely comprehensive.

As you trawl through however you're bound to be puzzled as to why some words – like flavour, colour – are spelt the American way. But not until you reach the end and click on some offered links, which plunge you into all manner of information about Spurgeon and other religious sites, do you start thinking, what's going on here? Even then the question is not answered. In the link 'Who is Phillip R.

Johnson?' where you'd confidently expect to get an explanation, there is no mention of Marmite...

There has to be a back-story. So I contacted Phil, executive director of Grace To You, a Christian tape and radio ministry, to try and get to the bottom of this Marmite mystery. The answer is simple. The good American preacher is as besotted with Marmite as he is with Spurgeon. And nowhere is it written that the two should never mix.

Here is his Marmite story: 'My first taste of Marmite was in 1984, in Bangalore, India. I was being hosted by the Australian dean of a theological college and his wife. They had a small jar of Marmite on the breakfast table. I was intrigued by it. I asked what it was and the dean's wife told me it was for spreading on toast. She encouraged me to try it, with a little butter. My expectation was that it would be something like apple butter – a dark, thick spread. Right? When I spread it and noticed it had the gooey consistency of honey, I thought, OK, this is a kind of molasses. My hostess politely cautioned me that I should not spread it thick, but she said no more than that. I rather like molasses, so I ignored her advice and slathered it on in abundance. I was fully expecting something sweet, so it was a serious shock – and an unpleasant surprise – when I tasted it. I asked for a more specific explanation of what it was and she explained that it was yeast extract and was savoury, not sweet. Since I had already coated my toast with it, I felt I ought to finish it. To my surprise, by the time I finished that first piece of toast, I was a fan. I've been eating it ever since. Once word got around that I liked it, friends from India, Australia, New Zealand, Singapore and Britain brought me large jars of it whenever they visited the US. So I have a lifetime supply stocked-up in one of our kitchen cabinets. The New Zealand variety is seriously inferior. My Aussie friends keep trying to convert me to **Vegemite**, which actually isn't bad but isn't as good as Marmite. The best is still the British original.' Amen!

Steel, Danielle: famed author of steamy 'beach' paperbacks, that now number 76 novels. What connection can she possibly have with the black goo? Her German grandfather 'invented' the American version! There's an American version? You bet - and it's called **Vegex**.

Switzerland: surprisingly, while not known for its beer production, it has 92 breweries. So, little wonder the Swiss have their own yeast extract. Called Cenovis, it has been around since 1931 when a group of Swiss brewers decided to piggy-back on the Marmite yeast-waste phenomenon. But Marmite could pick up a few ideas from Cenovis. It's available not only as a spread, but also as a powder and liquid seasoning. And the spread comes in jars and tubes, some of them very tiny which are perfect for travelling. And it also comes in a low-salt version.

Synaesthesia: the condition whereby on

hearing a particular word, a colour, and a certain image – not related to the word – is triggered. James Wannerton, president of the UK Synaesthesia Association, also 'tastes' words. He says it's best described as a 'union of the senses'. At the Association's 2008 conference in Edinburgh he made a speech in which he revealed that seeing a photo of George Brown '...leaves me with a very strong taste of dirt and Marmite...'. He tells me that white cars also give him a very strong Marmite taste, albeit Marmite mixed with butter. So what taste is triggered when he hears the word Marmite? 'It gives me a weak Marmite taste that's overwhelmed by something very much like semolina. Not too nice a combination, to be honest!' He was also keen to reveal another synaesthesia connection with Marmite. It was his inability to articulate the word 'expect' into real food terms. 'I had great difficulty in describing the taste and texture to myself, which can be pretty annoying. A bit like smelling something and not being able to remember what it is that smells like that. This was with me from childhood, up until a few years ago when I had some Marmite flavoured crisps. Bingo! That was the taste and texture I'd been agonising over for so long.'

Coincidentally, when James was interviewed for a BBC *Horizon* programme, Marmite came to the fore. Dr Jamie Ward, a neuro-psychologist, asked what taste he had when he heard the word 'might'. James told him: 'I get a strong Marmite flavour,' Next word up was 'wipe'. He answered: 'That's Marmite again.' And with 'light' – purposely picked because it rhymed with the previous two - Marmite again was James' response. But with an added taste: '...with lots of butter this time.' So, how does James feel about the real taste of it? 'I absolutely adore Marmite'. Thank goodness!

T

Taxi: Londoners and visitors to the capital will remember well the 33 taxis that, in 2002, were flamboyantly decorated with colourful Marmite **advertising** to celebrate the centenary. One side of the taxis proclaimed: '100 Years of Love', while the other side was emblazoned with: '100 years of Hate'. Like all advertising it ran its day and the Marmite cabs disappeared. One was preserved. Purchased by **Unilever** it now welcomes visitors to the Marmite factory in **Burton-on-Trent**. It's permanently parked outside the reception office.

Tankers: it's a surprising (make that surreal) sight – spotting a tanker truck zooming down a motorway with a huge image of a jar of Marmite emblazoned on both sides and the rear. In fact it's something of a shock. It's just not the way fans expect to see the object of their passion being transported. Maybe it would be a more acceptable sight if it bore a fun slogan. Something on the lines of: coming to a jar near you...

Having said that, the mess inside the tanker is nowhere near ready for a jar. It's not processed Marmite — it's the yeast-sludge, being transported from breweries all over the country, to the Marmite factory in **Burton-on-Trent**. In the trade it's called 'slurry'. I know, not quite as romantic as we all thought. Though the 'loathers' will get a kick out of it.

Tar-in-a-jar: the nickname bestowed on Marmite by my American husband, Gary. When trying to win him over, score a point or get him to do something, I wave an open jar under his nose. He hates everything about it so much he's instantly putty. And, reportedly, that's pretty much the 'game' singer Amy Winehouse's pals forced her to play in 2009, in a bid to drive the thought of that then wayward, now ex-husband Blake Fielder-Civil, out of her mind. Every time Amy mentioned his name, pals of the pop star, made her strip-down to her skivvies, snort a line of innocent sherbert, then wolf down two Jaffa

cakes smothered in Marmite! It worked...
Shortly afterwards they divorced.

Another example of how Marmite has its 'do
as I say' uses comes from Emma Bird, who
runs the *How To Italy* website, that helps
expats cope with the bureaucracy of moving to
Italy or doing business there. Emma, from
Poole, Dorset, fell in love with her adopted
country while teaching English on the island of
Sardina. In October 2008 she blogged about
the 'secret weapon' she used to keep her
students in-line. She used Marmite. 'It's the
most effective weapon there is in keeping
everyone, from lively kids to gossiping adults,
disciplined,' she reported.

'When they're not focusing on the English task
in hand, I take the Marmite out of my bag,
place it on my desk and unscrew the top. The
effect is instant silence, without me having to
say anything. And that's not because I put the
fear of God into them: it's because the brown
stuff does.' She also revealed that one of her
students had begged for a jar, so she could
use the Marmite-technique at home, when her
six-year-old twin sons were kicking-up.

It works. For some. As members of
Mumsnet.com know. One frantic mother
turned to the website chat forum for help in
stopping her four-year-old son biting his two-
year-old sister. Another answered promptly
with her solution: 'We stopped it with
Marmite,' she revealed. Every time her young
son bit, he had his tongue dabbed with it. 'It
stopped the biting within a couple of weeks,'

she reported. The downside? 'It gave him a lifetime phobia of Marmite.' But there's obviously a 50/50 chance that this forcible feeding of Marmite will not work. And the kid could end up biting even more – to ensure a steady supply of that so-tasty 'punishment'!

Testing: there's constant debate and argument – and real humdinger rows – between devotees of the various yeast extracts out there. The rift between Marmite and **Vegemite** followers can deeply affect relationships. The question: which one is best? is impossible to answer. Unless you're in that rare position of not having a dog in the fight! So who better to turn to for an unbiased opinion, than someone from Japan. Enter Makiko Itoh, who was born in Tokyo, has lived in Britain and the States, and is now a resident of Switzerland. Her real job is web-design, she's the author of JavaScript + CSS+DOM Magic, and a frequent speaker at international conferences. But her passion is food, which she expresses through her website *justhungry.com*. In 2006 Makiko subjected Marmite, **Vegemite** and the Swiss version of yeast extract Cenovis, to a personal taste-test. In the end she had to admit to a slight bias, having spent some of her childhood in Britain eating Marmite sandwiches. But despite that, Marmite only just squeezed into her number one spot, on the basis it was stronger tasting than the others with a 'sort of meaty taste'. Her second choice was the Swiss rival. 'I must say that

Cenovis is surprisingly tasty,' was her verdict. 'It has an adult air to it, due to a beer undertone.' As for Vegemite, Makiko had nothing good to say about it. 'My least favourite by far,' she pronounced. It had a 'very slightly fishy taste, plus the taste of desiccated onion flakes. It just doesn't do it at all for me.' She feared her dismissal of it would get her banned from entering 'that great nation of Australia'.

Thermal: geeks who run out of thermal grease or paste, while building computers, or anything else that relies of the conduction of heat between two pieces of metal, have been known to reach for the Marmite jar. Evidently it's preferred to the other emergency standbys, such as toothpaste and peanut butter.

Theory: there are plenty of theories about Marmite, some fun, some plain stupid, but none as wonderfully silly as the one highlighted by an American living in Sheffield. Jamie Charlotte Mitchell, from Seattle, Washington State, has taken to Marmite as though to the taste born. JC, as she likes to be known, has a website on which she writes reviews of her two favourite pastimes: drinking beer and coffee; sometimes at the same time, But she's also used it to post her Marmite Theory of Migratory Evolution.

It's based on the way she claims so many everyday, household items don't get returned to the place where they are supposed to be. JC, a librarian, theorised 'this law' applies to, among other things, pens, scissors, remote controls, key sections of the newspaper, telephone directories, sharp knives, cordless phones, reading glasses and shopping lists. But so the entire contents of a house are prevented from becoming 'a churning cauldron of omni-directional chaos' she claims there are a few constants that are destined to return to the same place, no matter how far they are moved. Among these are: the dog bowl and the Marmite.

The next time she visits her mother in Seattle she will put the theory to the test. She is sure that the jar of Marmite she took with her on the last trip home will still be there, just where she left it, as she told me: 'Sitting unnoticed on my mother's kitchen counter, quietly controlling the movement of all temporarily misplaced articles in the universe.'

Thiamin: is Vitamin B-1 and essential for the heart and the central nervous system to function correctly and is required to metabolise carbohydrates. It's found in concentrated amounts in yeast and is the property that starts the fermenting process. A deficiency is dire and causes beriberi, the disease that killed so many **POWs** held by the Japanese. They suffered so terribly because they got little more than 'polished' rice to survive on. The process strips the rice of its natural outer layer of thiamin. The same happens when grains are processed, which is why in many countries white loafs and white flour products are fortified with thiamin.

Truffles: the chocolate variety, filled with Marmite! See **Young**, Paul A.

Tunisia: another example of how putting 'Marmite' into a search engine, can plunge you into a totally unrelated world. And a very informative one to boot. The website *No Marmite in Tunisia* comes up, high on the pecking order, when searching for info about the spread. While it will tell you nothing about Marmite, it will give you a lot of information about living the expat life in that North African country. Shortly after Melanie Benna quit life in Ramsgate to move to her husband's home country, she decided to create a website – in a bid to counteract her loneliness by making contact with other Brits living in Tunisia. But what to call it? The Marmite link popped into her head very quickly. 'I thought it would be a fun and whacky name, something that would not be forgotten easily,' she told me. 'Also, every story, article or report I had ever read about Brits moving abroad included the question of whether they could get hold of Marmite!' The website did the trick. Melanie now counts many other expats among her friends. She regularly updates her website, with stories and articles about her travels around her adopted country. She's also started a second website – selling Tunisian properties to foreigners. And anyone who goes out to inspect one of the white-washed villas she's handling should know what gift to take for Melanie.

Twiglets: hands up those who know that Twiglets do not contain Marmite? We all assume they do. How wrong we are! Twiglets – those crunchy, hard-baked, twiggy-looking snacks, with a distinct Marmitey taste – have been around almost as long as Marmite. They were first produced by Peek Frean in 1929 for the Christmas market. But their popularity was so enormous they've been made ever since. And like Marmite, Twiglets have taken on iconic status. So if they have a Marmite taste, how come they're not made with it? Well they are, at least as close as can be without actually using it. The generic form of Marmite (yeast extract) is the flavouring. A wonderful story surely hovers over the 'invention' of Twiglets, one that echoes with industrial espionage, commercial betrayal, or both...

Peek Frean's archives have sparse information on the history of Twiglets. All presumably lost, or trashed, when Peek Freans was taken over by Jacob's, which is now owned by United Biscuits. The only details anyone connected with the production of the 80-year-old snack, now made in Aintree, knows is that the Marmitey-mind behind them was Peek Frean's technical manager, a Frenchman called Rondalin. His first name is unknown. Monsieur Rondalin came up with the concept of adding yeast extract to the nobbly 'twig', that emerged while he was experimenting with the dough that made the company's original best-seller, Vita-Wheat. And as he was French, it begs the question: did Monsieur Rondalin have inside knowledge of the secret of how Marmite was made? Was he in on the original formula, that his fellow countryman Louis Pasteur came up with? Did he miss out on the patenting of the formula that was finally sold to the Brits in 1902? Did he exact his revenge with Twiglets? I attempted to get the true history of Twiglets out of Jacobs and United Biscuits, but all they could come up with was: 'Twiglets are made from a yeast extract, similar to the Marmite taste.' So, next time you pop a Twiglet, ponder on the mystery of the mysterious Monsieur Rondalin!

U

Umami: it was always thought that there were four primary tastes: sweet, sour, salt and bitter. But there is a fifth. It's 'umami' — best defined as the 'yummy' or 'amazing' factor. Marmite is loaded with it. As is soy sauce, green tea, seaweed, truffles and — wait for it… mothers' breast milk. Although isolated by the Japanese in 1908, umami (in Japanese it roughly translates to 'tasty') is only now being recognised by the culinary and eating world at large. But for decades the artificial version has been around. MSG (monosodium glutamate) is the chemical derivative of glutamate, which is naturally occurring in products that fall into the umami category.

Yeast extract is one of them.

Hence the Marmite umami overload.

"...and for the umami touch I'm adding Marmite."

To really underline how Marmite is one of the best deliveries of that fifth taste, top British chef Sat Bains went to Japan to demonstrate how marvellous Marmite is in cooking. Sharing the umami limelight with him was another highly-rated chef, Claude Bosi of Hibiscus in London. They were invited by the Umami Information Center, which is headquartered in Tokyo, to take part in a dietary education class that highlighted umami, given to 40 high school pupils, in the ancient capital of Kyoto. Claude used Lea and Perrins Worcestershire Sauce, on a combo Parmesan and Cheddar toastie. Sat – who has been hailed as the most inventive British chef of his generation – showed the teenagers how to use Marmite, to add that certain something. He'd slow cooked, for 24 hours, a joint of pork rib, using the vacuum-bag technique, which he then sliced into 8mm thin strips before sautéing in a non-stick pan. In the final moments of cooking he brushed Marmite onto each strip. The kids raved about the 'wow' taste the finishing touch put to the pork. As the Umami Information Center put it: 'The Marmite was a perfect match for the rich, aromatic flavour of the sautéed pork.'

They didn't have to tell Sat that's how it would work. He knew only too well. Marmite is one of his favourite things to cook with. And many of the dishes he creates at his famed Restaurant Sat Bains with Rooms in Nottingham – it boasts a Michelin One Star rating – owe their taste to a smear, a dash or a dollop. 'I always put Marmite in my stews, the ragouts and bolognaise,' he told me. 'It adds a real hit of umami.' Marmite even gets a mention on the menu, which features pan-fried Cornish brill, Marmite and texture of onions. So how does that work on fish? 'I just brush the Marmite on the brill as it comes out of the pan. It's the only seasoning used – it adds such a depth of flavour.'

Sat also gets another kick out of using Marmite. 'I love it when people ask me what that wonderful flavour is in a certain dish and I tell them it's Marmite. So many of then say: "no way – I hate Marmite".' As for his own

Marmite eating habits he admitted to one food treat he has never tried. 'I've never had Marmite on toast. I was born in Britain but my parents were from the Punjab and Marmite was something I never encountered until I started cooking. And now it's part of my life because of the intensity it can add to so many dishes. It's quite an amazing product.'

Undercoat: Many artists, modellers – even Hollywood set designers – know the Marmite secret. It's used as a secondary undercoat, in areas where a weathered or antique look needs to be created. Marmite is evidently useful because it dissolves in warm water. It's painted over and, once dried, the item being worked on is either soaked, or scrubbed down, in warm water. The Marmite layer softens and disappears and the desired look emerges. This bizarre technique was confirmed by American Scott Ferguson, owner of the California-based Marmite Pantry. He tells me he had a customer who told him, 'you will never guess what I use Marmite for…'. And he went onto to tell Scott that he was an art instructor and also worked as a movie set painter. He used Marmite as an undercoat in the spots he wanted to look worn. After the top layer dried, the Marmite was washed out and the result looked like it was old and peeling. Scott recalled: 'I told him, you're right – I've never heard of that before!'

Underground: not the tube, not below sea level, but the restaurant. The Underground is a leader in the phenomena of the illegal eatery craze. This is all to do with folk opening-up their dining-rooms in a very public, but private, way. Among the first to do this in Britain was a woman in Kilburn, North London. She doesn't want to reveal her name in case the nosey-parker, red-tape Gods bust her and her 'speakeasy' diner. She operates under her blog/web/twittering-name of *Msmarmitelover*. As she explained to me: 'I chose *Msmarmitelover* because I am actually a marmite baby, brought up on the stuff, love it. But also because it's hard to think of an original address when you are signing up to be a blogger. This one just sprung up in my mind.' To prove she has a constant interest in Marmite, the sideboard in the dining room of her home, where the 'illegal' diners gather, has an array of Marmite jars. And to show that her interest is real she has held a Marmite-themed evening – when every dish featured the black-stuff as an ingredient.

In June, 2009, she served 30 paying guests with a five course dinner, each one featuring Marmite. The courses were: M on linseed toast points; M-baked mushrooms in thyme and garlic butter; rocket/spinach/watercress salad with an M and lime vinaigrette; M-smeared grated Cheddar cheese-covered, smoked haddock, with M-roasted tomatoes; coffee ice-cream with chocolate-M-sauce. She conceded it was not the easiest dinner she's prepared. 'The menu was rather daunting,' she confessed later. 'My approach was to use Marmite as a seasoning, as a replacement for salt. It is such a strong, distinctive taste and I was conscious of one guest writing to me, only half joking, saying that he would bring his high blood-pressure medicine, just in case.'

The Marmite fare went down very well – and to great compliments. It surprised some by being so edible! That was the verdict of one couple who signed-up for the dinner, clearly not having taken note of the 'theme', and admitted on arrival they hated Marmite. And the hostess was really surprised that even after so much Marmite-infused food several of the diners went for the mug of hot Marmite, instead of coffee, at the end. As she pointed out: 'Now that's loving it!' An extra special treat, as a final flourish, was provided by a VIP guest, who sent everyone home with a sample of his gourmet speciality (see **Young, Paul A**)...

Unilever: Marmite is just one of 400 food, household and personal care brands owned by Unilever. It came under Unilever control in 2000, joining such diverse products as Domestos bleach, Pond's face cream and Ben and Jerry's ice-cream. Unilever is an Anglo-Dutch corporation, with its global headquarters in Rotterdam. The CEO, Paul Polman, is Dutch. Unilever came into being with the 1930 merger of British soapmaker Lever Brothers and Dutch margarine producer Margarine Unie. The conglomerate has 174,000 employees in 100 countries.

University: how life at these great schools of learning prepare one for life! Particularly for those who have the privilege of studying at Cambridge. As was revealed in June 2009, there is a certain 'test' that has to be undergone to prove you are fit for the real world and it's got nothing to do with finals. It follows the inconvenience of those pesky exams and occurs when the fun and games of what is dubbed 'Suicide Sunday' takes over. In among the massive binge-drinking chaos, there are certain initiation ceremonies that have to be survived. Chief among them is drinking through a fish smeared in Marmite! And as the drink is non-alcoholic, there's no help from the liquid intake to get down what sounds like a desperately foul concoction.

USA: the feelings of many Americans – and probably a fair number of Brits – have been lyrically expressed by Warren Hoge, a former London bureau chief for the *New York Times*. As Marmite's centenary approached, he wrote a feature in which he pointed out that there were two very special 2002 British celebrations. One was the silver jubilee of the Queen, the other was commemorating the 100th year of the country coming under the rule of another 'strange' British institution: Marmite. He wrote that it had: 'a toxic odour, saline taste and an axle grease consistency, that has somehow captivated the British... it's enshrined as a national symbol, right up there with the royal family and the Sunday roast... that no foreigner has ever been known to like;

it simply adds to its domestic allure and its iconic status as an emblem of enduring British insularity and bloody-mindedness. Were Hogarth to paint a still life of a 21st century British pantry, a jar of Marmite would have to figure in it...'

V

Vauxhall: nothing to do with the motor car. But a lot to do with the once-upon-a-time manufacture of Marmite. The London neighbourhood used to be home to a Marmite factory. In 1927 a disused building in Durham Street, appropriately once a brewery, was converted to accommodate the overflow business from **Burton-on-Trent**. Some days the stench that came from the factory was so awful that nearby residents campaigned to get a reduction in their rates. They were not successful.

The Vauxhall factory churned out Marmite until 1954 when all production was transferred into a new purpose built facility in Burton. After Marmite moved out the Vauxhall factory lay dormant until 1969, when it finally found a new use – as London's first hostel for the homeless. It was opened by St Mungo's and marked its debut as a the most pro-active charity for down-and-outs.

Vegemite: the opposition! It was 'invented' in 1923 as the Australian rival to Marmite. The two taste quite different. Unlike Marmite it does not contain the health-promoting vitamin B-12 (see **Cyanocobalamin**). One popular belief is that the Aussies came up with Vegemite because their pride determined that anything the Brits could do, they could do too, and better. But the truth is much more salient. During World War I, like so many other imported products, supplies of Marmite to Australia were severely restricted. Fred Walker, owner of a quickly growing Melbourne food company, decided the best way round the shortage was to produce his own. But the Marmite recipe was a closely guarded secret. And the British owners were of no help, even if they had wanted to be. In something of a rash decision, they had parted with both the name and the formula to a New Zealand company (see **Sanitarium**), and the exclusive rights agreement was for Australasia... So Fred set his chief chemist, Dr Cyril Callister, to work – to come up with an Aussie version. It took him several years of research to come up with the right formula. Some would say it's still not right...

Vegemite got its name as the result of a competition in which Walker's daughter, Sheilah pulled the name out of a hat. But the name did nothing to boost sales. Despite the publicity surrounding the shipment that had been sent to Thursday Island to combat an epidemic outbreak of beriberi, sales remained sluggish. Marmite was easily available again and Vegemite was vegetating. Another naming competition was held. The old joke, 'mar-might, but pa-will' was the basis for the winning suggestion – Parwill. Whoever came up with that bright idea is lost in the Marmitey mists of time. Maybe they wanted their identity to be lost, because the imitation Marmite fared no better when it was sold as Parwill! Before long the name Vegemite was re-installed. Then came World War II and more shortages of products from the 'old country' – which allowed Vegemite to get a nationalistic strangle-hold as strong as Marmite is on Britain. Now, like its British counterpart, Vegemite is owned by a giant conglomerate: Kraft Foods. And, again like Marmite, it faces challenges from alternative yeast extracts. One of them is British Marmite, which Down Under has to trade as Our Mate – because of the aforementioned deal with the Kiwis.

Vegetarians: Marmite is a mainstay for non-meat eaters. But not all vegetarians embrace it. Many boycott it because they do not like the idea that Marmite shares factory premises with **Bovril**. **Unilever**, owner of both, stresses that during production the products never meet. And it's curious that the factory displays only a Marmite sign in the shape of a giant jar on top of an ageing water tower. Perhaps it's something to do with the less that consumers know...?

Vegetarians-2: dogs, while largely seen as carnivorous, survive very well as vegetarians. The Vegetarian Society emphasises the use of

Marmite in a doggy-veggie-diet. Apart from feeding Rover Marmite sandwiches they also suggest adding it to textured soya protein, to 'make it more attractive for them'.

Vegex: the American yeast extract, is little heard of, even over there, but it has a staunch and loyal following. It is the oldest yeast extract in the world, after Marmite which is older by only eight years. Vegex was the 'invention' of Julius Schuelein, a German lawyer who turned to chemistry in a bid to unlock the secrets of used brewer's yeast. His interest in turning it into an edible form was sparked by his family's involvement in the brewing industry. In 1895, his father Josef founded the Union Brewery in Munich, which eventually after many amalgamations became part of the giant Lowenbrau beer company.

In the late-thirties, John Schuelein, son of

Julius, joined the huge wave of German-Jewish immigrants who started a new life in America, where Vegex was already well established. It got a mention in the *Modern Meatless Cook Book,* published in the US in 1910; the US anti-vivisection organisation The Millenium Guild staged a vegetarian Thanksgiving dinner in 1913, at the famous Copley Hotel in Boston, where Vegex was served for the soup course; in 1920 the *Vegex Cookery Book* came out. John formed the Vitamin Food Company – with Vegex as its leading product – and Americanized his name by adding 'Steel' to it. In 1947 he had a daughter: the famed novelist Danielle Steel.

Like Marmite, Vegex was marketed on its health-giving properties, particularly for children. One early advertisement shows a two-year-old at the dining table eating a slice of bread and Vegex. The main caption claims: 'She is Taller, Heavier, More Advanced than the Average Child of Her Age.' And in smaller print it reveals: 'Her parents ascribe this unusual development to the use of Vegex...'

In the 1920s cookery book, the forward reads: 'The gift of health cannot be measured by price. Day by day we learn more and more about the intimate relation between good health and right living. And the most important part of right living is our daily food. Unless the diet contains the right amounts of mineral and organic salts and vitamins, true health can hardly be possible. Too many of the modern foods are refined to a point where the vital essentials are lost and any diet poor in these essentials is bound to have an injurious effect on bodily well being. But there is a food, VEGEX, palatable, tempting, appetizing which puts back into the diet those vital elements man has taken out of foods by civilized foolishness. VEGEX is purely a vegetable product, concentrated from specially cultured yeast. Of all food in the world, it is the richest in the valuable Vitamin-B. It bears the endorsement of the world's great food and dietetic experts, scientific institutions, sanatoriums and health foundations.'

Those words stand in endorsement of any yeast extract as much today as they did all those years ago. Now Vegex has added a special group of people it helps. Since 1999 it's been owned by the Center for Educational Advancement. A non-profit, based in Flemington, New Jersey, all proceeds from Vegex go to fund programmes for people with special needs. In fact - along with several other products - it is packed and distributed by the the people it benefits. So, while Vegex does its American consumers good, it empowers and employs the disadvantaged who get it to them.

Vinaigrette: to the traditional mix of olive oil/vinegar/lemon juice/garlic/mustard, throw in a teaspoon of Marmite.

To ensure the 'loathers' love it... just don't tell them about the 'secret' ingredient.

Vitamins: Marmite packs a punch. Particularly when it comes to the Bs – as in **Thiamin**, **Riboflavin**, **Niacin**, **Folic acid** and **Cyanocobalamin**.

Vows: now that couples routinely write their own wedding vows, it can only be a matter of time before a Marmite loathing bride or 'groom looks into the eyes of their Marmite lover and intones: 'I promise to love and cherish you, to hold from this day forward – and start eating Marmite – for better or worse.'

W

Waldron: Sean Waldron is, without a doubt, the Marmite website-meister. He's the founder and keeper of: *www.ilovemarmite.com* and *www.ihatemarmite.com*. The story of how he became involved is a good example of how, if you see a chance, grab it. In 2000 Sean was working in IT research and development in the States. Occasionally he would be asked by American friends and colleagues about Marmite which was, and still is, perceived as a peculiarly British product. He would refer them to the Marmite website – under the mistaken perception that there was one. He checked and found little if anything. 'I found one page,' he told me. 'And that was asking whether fans of Marmite would like a website!' In disbelief that there was nothing more substantial on the internet he searched further. 'I tried "I love Marmite" and found nothing. I tried "I hate Marmite" and also found nothing. Five minutes later I was the proud owner of both domains.'

Sean, who is now back in Britain, chuckled at what has happened since: 'I do like Marmite, but would never have said I was an expert, although I've turned into a bit of one now.' You can say that again! He has been interviewed about his site and his knowledge of Marmite by media outlets all over the world and many of those articles and broadcasts have been syndicated. 'As a result I have received messages from the most unlikely places, where people have read about me, or heard me interviewed,' he said.

The chances are that you might also hear about Sean because of his non-Marmite life. He is an amazingly talented jiver and jive teacher. He was introduced to the revival of the dance, which was the ballroom craze of the 50s and 60s, while living in Boston, Massachusetts. He now owns three modern-jive dance schools in London and Buckinghamshire. Surprisingly he's not come up yet with a dance called The Marmite...

Waste: from waste-to-waste... that's the life of the Marmite production line. It starts with the leftovers from brewing and ends up with vats full of liquid waste. At least the beginning of the process is a fantastic feat of recycling but the same cannot be said about the last part, which has now got a reputation for causing a bit of a stink. In the summer of 2009 it was revealed that the Marmite liquid by-product was being dumped in a field in the Derbyshire village of Sawley, 53 miles from the Marmite factory. Ostensibly it was supposed to be a fertilizer. But whatever, it caused two stinks: one from the waste itself, the other raised by the villagers.

For two months the residents of Sawley kicked-up a stink about the stink. Finally, after a petition and a community meeting, the folk responsible were forced into action by the Environment Agency. The recycling contractor, White's of Grantham, refuse to discuss the problem, while a Marmite spokesman was widely quoted as saying simply: 'The site will no longer be used for the disposal of the waste.' Which begs the questions: where was it being dumped for the previous 100-plus years... and where is it being dumped now?

Something of an answer probably lies in the fact that in October 2008 the sewage pipes serving the Marmite factory in Burton-on-Tent, started spewing filth into a site close by. It turned out the pipes were corroded and the years and years of Marmite waste passing through them was blamed. People were not happy. Particularly unhappy was the DIY store, B&Q; the contaminated site was where they'd just built a new super-store. The opening was delayed for 11 months. But it was Delora Jones – she lives just a sniff away from the factory – who first raised the signal that the waste was becoming a serious problem. In 2003 she was tired of complaining about the dreadful odour that invaded her life and that of her neighbours and went public. American-born Delora, who has lived in **Burton-on-Trent** since 1996, told the *Burton Mail*: 'People think having a good sense of smell is a blessing. But here, in Burton, it is a curse!' Later she discovered that the sewage system was not adequate to cope with the waste and that an effluent tower had been built to resolve the problem. But that turned out not to be air-tight. In a bid to stem the smell Marmite announced they had 'renewed' the peat and heather filter beds in the waste plant, but added that at the end of the day it was a manufacturing site and therefore could not be made completely smell-free. Since Delora complained so publicly, the stench has disappeared to such an extent that she's started eating Marmite again. 'I was so fed up with the Marmite factory and the people in charge I stopped buying it,' she told me. 'But now it's so much better, nowhere near as bad as it was, I've started eating it again.' Clearly the stink had been transferred to Sawley! But where is it now?

Websites: there are several Marmite websites. There's the official one, operated by **Unilever**, plus the one cited under **Waldron**. And two others that are perfect examples of how bizarrely Marmite comes into our lives - because they are both off-shoots of subjects enormously removed from Marmite. (See **Accomodata** and **Spurgeon**.)

White: the colour Marmite turns when beaten! Go on, try it. By a miracle of physics it will turn white. Not pristine, gleaming, pure white, but close. I started hammering away at about 100grams with a wooden spoon. Almost instantly it started turning. I gave out a whoop because, although I'd known about the theory for years, I felt it might just be something of a silly old tale. Within two minutes, as the almost black glob took on the look of pumpkin-pie mix, I'd had enough: arthritis and beating Marmite do not go together! So I let a hand-held electric whisk take over. Hey ho, within a couple of minutes the Marmite was unrecognisable. It had practically doubled in amount, looked like cappuccino, was fluffy on the tongue and tasted somewhat less salty.

It's said there is a Marmite Beaters' Club out there. I've found no trace of it. But the magic colour change was first broadcast to the world, quite literally, on the much lamented *Home Truths*, the BBC Radio 4 programme hosted by the late and wonderful John Peel. Not long after, that other late and wonderful BBC personality Ned Sherrin, got some of his guests banging on about beating Marmite, on *Loose Ends*, another Radio 4 production.

So what is the point? Well, there is a science lesson here. It is well explained on *www.MadSci.org,* which is promoted as 'the laboratory that never sleeps'. In 1998 a Bristol University chemistry student posed the question: 'why does Marmite turn white when patted repeatedly with a spoon?' The answer came from the other side of the world. Professor John Christie of the School of Chemistry, at La Trobe University, Melbourne, posted the reply. He explained it was all to do with its 'visco-elastic flow properties'. He then went on to talk about how beating the Marmite roughens the surface into 'a tangle of microscopic peaks and valleys', which in turn increases the amount of surface reflection, which means that the light we see coming from it… oh, I give up! But the good professor confirmed it turned white. And in a message to me he explained, in a much easier way, what happens. 'I notice on checking the answer I posted, that I mention visco-elasticity. That is a complicated concept, but not a totally unfamiliar one. The best way of illustrating this is to think what happens when you beat normal liquid, like water. It flies all over the place. But beat an egg, which is a visco-elastic liquid, and it wraps around the whisk.' In his posted message the Aussie professor had a joke at the expense of his British questioner: 'I wouldn't trust a breakfast spread that does this. Perhaps you should change to Vegemite!'

To my mind the best thing about knowing this – that it does turn white, not why it does – is the fun and games you can have. Ask a friend (a good one) if they'd like to sample the 'crème caramel' you've prepared for a dinner party. Then stand back and wait for your friend to start spluttering... with pleasure, or perhaps not.

Withers: wither thy **Marmart** now, Wayne (see **Art**)? When Wayne Withers bought the squeezy Marmite art-on-toast collection, he said he wanted to give his wife Lisa a Christmas gift 'that nobody else has'. He said he owned a sandwich shop in New Tredegar, South Wales, but in fact he just worked in one, part-time. What he also didn't reveal was that he'd funded the purchase of the Marmart collection with ill-gotten gains, to the extent that on the day he planned to give his wife her unique Christmas gift he was in jail. He was found guilty of selling counterfeit DVDs on e-Bay, the same auction site he bought the Marmart. In a two month period he raked in £5,355 from his illegal operation. He was sentenced to 16 weeks in jail.

So, once he was toast in the eyes of the law,

what happened to the toast art he paid £920 for? 'I still have it,' Wayne confirmed to me. 'It's framed and hanging on my living-room wall.' So it wasn't confiscated as part of his punishment? 'No – the money I bought it with had nothing to do with what landed me in jail,' he insisted. Wayne, who now lives in Penydarren, Merthyr Tydfil and still makes sandwiches for a living, said his wife was 'shocked' when he gave her the unique 'art', which he did before going to jail. As for any visitors to his home, he has an easy answer when they ask: 'Why have you got all that toast on your wall?' He shows them articles about the Marmart, that he's framed. One assumes that both Wayne and his wife, or at least her, are rabid consumers of the 'paint' used for the toast portraits. But surprisingly that is not the case. 'We're both the same... we like Marmite a little bit. Just now and then, spread ever so thinly.'

Wooden crates: there are some of the wooden crates that jars of Marmite used to be packed in and delivered to grocery shops still around... So, when you're clearing out the attic, the garage, the shed, or the glory-hole under the stairs and you find one, hang onto it for dear life! They're rare finds, and rapidly increasing in value. Apart from that, they make wonderful decorative touches: put a plant in it, use it as a display case for your other Marmite memorabilia, and they provide a terrific topic of conversation. The history on them is murky, but they probably date back to the earliest days of Marmite and come in two sizes: one that held a dozen 2oz jars, and another for a dozen 1 oz jars.

Clive Cunningham, a retired boat-builder of Lancing, West Sussex, was delighted to unearth one of the 2oz-size boxes when he was clearing-out his late father-in-law's shed. It was full of rusty nails. Apart from cleaning it up he hasn't done anything special with the box and doubts he will. But he knows he'll never part with it. 'I couldn't bear to get rid of it,' he told me. 'Not because I'm mad about Marmite but just because it represents a world that has disappeared."

Woolton Pie: the most famous of the World War II recipes was conjured up in a bid to make tasty dishes out of limited food supplies. The official recipe called for 'vegetable-extract' but that meant just one thing: Marmite. And very quickly, whenever the recipe was repeated, Marmite was substituted for 'vegetable-extract'. The pie was a mixture of potato, swede, cauliflower, carrot and spring onion, thickened with Marmite-flavoured oatmeal, then covered with a layer of potato or wholemeal pastry. It was created by Francois Latry, head chef of the Savoy Hotel. He called it Woolton Pie after Frederick Marquis, Lord Woolton, who was head of the Ministry of Food, during those dark days. It was unveiled in a report in *The Times*, on September 26th 1941. In recent times, thanks to the recession and a renewed interest in how people coped in those food-austere times, mention of Woolton Pie (invariably with Marmite as an ingredient) has popped up all over the place.

Worms: eat Marmite like a kid! Spread butter and Marmite on a Ryvita then press a second Ryvita on top – and watch all the Marmite worms come wriggling through the holes! After you've stopped playing with it, eat it.

Worrall Thompson: (Antony), celebrity chef. What a brave man. He took on the might of Marmite and and lost. In September 2007 he launched Toastmate, his own version of yeast extract. But the name he came up with was something of a self-fulfilling prophecy. As in: you're toast, mate! Mid-2009, while still struggling to overcome the well reported financial hit he'd taken during the credit-crunch, he called it quits. He told me that he'd been motivated to enter the tough yeast extract spread market in a bid to help people cut-back on their sodium intake. At launch it was touted as being 25% lower than Marmite's. AWT claims that as a result Marmite's sodium level was reduced. At the close of play the standings were: Toastmate 3.1grams per 100grams, opposed to Marmite's 3.9grams. Toastmate found its fans – among those who could actually find it – but it lacked the power of **advertising**. As AWT said 'Unless you're prepared to put millions behind a massive advertising campaign it's very difficult to take on the big-boys.'

Wreaths: when celebrity phenomenon Jade

Goody died in 2009, she got what she had requested at her funeral: a wreath shaped like a Marmite jar. She said it would symbolise how people felt about her: loved her, or hated her. But she was not the first to have the mighty-M as an integral part of a funeral. That tragic honour went to a university student who died in 2007. But the reason he got a Marmite look-alike floral tribute was for a very distinctly different reason: he loved the stuff and practically lived on it. His aunt, who was aware of his predilection for Marmite – 'he survived on it,' she said – ordered the Marmite wreath. She got her good friend florist Donna Woolston, who owns Florum, in the historic and charming Essex village of Coggeshall, to make it. 'It was the hardest floral-arrangement challenge I've ever had,' she told me. But she pulled it off with tremendous style using red carnations and yellow chrysanthemums. But the black jar? To achieve that authentic look Donna turned to a trick of the trade. 'There are no black flowers, so I used a special paint that we use for special effects.'

X

Xató: a typical Catalan dish. Xató is a sauce made with almonds, hazelnuts, breadcrumbs, vinegar, garlic, and black pepper. Traditionally it's served over an endive salad. And how do the Ex-pat Brits around Barcelona liven it up just a little? You've guessed it...

X-Rated: make that 'XX'. If you really want to know how Marmite is perceived, by some, consult the internet Urban Dictionary and put Marmite into 'search'. Just ensure you have the parental-control on. This is, after all, a family-friendly book, and the entries have no place in a volume primarily about food.

X-Rated 2: but, despite referring to this as a family book, I can't resist revealing that a big percentage of Marmite-lovers love to put it on their lovers, instead of on toast! In a poll taken on *www.ilovemarmite.com* the second most favourite way of eating it was when it was used in sex-games! Voters were asked to vote on when Marmite is Best.

The results: on toast, 56%; licked off my partner, 27%; straight from the pot, 11%; as a drink, 4%.

Y

Yearning: the feeling that comes over those separated from their beloved spread, when they know there's no hope of dipping a knife, or finger, into that gooey, salty, dark-brown mush, anytime soon. This feeling was best summed-up by Paul Ridout, who was kidnapped while back-packing in India, in 1994. The first thing he did on getting back to Britain, after being released by Kashmiri separatists who held him for several weeks, was to dive into Marmite on toast. He then provided the finest testimony to Marmite ever uttered. 'It's just one of those things – you get out of the country and it's all you can think about.'

Yearning-2: legendary train robber Ronnie Biggs had his yearning satisfied as soon as he gave himself up. For the long flight home in 2001 – after more than 30 years on the run in Brazil – the plane, chartered by the *Sun* newspaper, which returned him into the hands of British justice for his part in the 1963 Great Train Robbery, carried what Ronnie had missed most: British beer, a curry – and Marmite.

Yeast: is an organism that is 50% protein. Without it there would be no beer and therefore no Marmite. So what is it? To start with there is not just one yeast, there are hundreds of them. But they share a common bond in that they are all unicellular fungi. There are 100,000 different types of fungus, and fall into four divisions. Yeasts come under 'ascomycota', which accounts for 75% of all fungi, including lichen, mildews, black mould and the species that cause Dutch elm disease, chestnut blight and apple scab. On a happier note it also the division that is home to morels and truffles. The yeast chiefly used for alcoholic fermentation thus becoming the starter for Marmite, is *saccharomyces cerevisiae*, which gets its name from a combination of Latin and ancient Greek for 'sugar mould' and 'of beer'.

Yellow: has been a prominent part of the Marmite livery ever since 1928, when it was put in dark glass jars. It's the colour of the lid, the label surround and the picture of the French marmite cooking pot, on it. A good friend, Heather Stanton, of Newcastle upon Tyne, has a nice take on the yellow factor in the Marmite artwork. 'I eat Marmite only in the winter,' she says. 'It's all to do with the comfort it provides on those dark grim mornings. I crawl out of bed, let the dog out, put the kettle on. Then I open the kitchen cupboard to get the Marmite out – and there's that lovely yellow lid, smiling at me!'

You: 'have a face like a crumpet smeared with Marmite'… If anyone tells you that, take it as a compliment, because it puts you in the same category of good looks as BBC star news-reader George Alagiah. The *Mail on Sunday*, on August 4 2009, reported that Terry Wogan hurled the 'insult' at George during his morning Radio 2 show. It was not an original comment: a listener had sent it in, for Terry to use in any banter he wanted to engage in with Sri-Lankan born George.

Young, Paul A: He's a splendid example of how, increasingly, gourmet personalities regard Marmite with mighty respect. As a top chocolate creator you'd expect Paul to offer the finest and most imaginative combinations, to tickle and satisfy the most fickle of taste buds. And so he does. But among his more delectable selections – from the traditional strawberry fillings to the extraordinary red wine-soaked prunes – is a Marmite filled truffle. It is one of his most popular offerings. It became even more popular after a guest appearance at the Marmite-themed dinner at the 'illegal' **Underground**, when he handed out his Marmite-chocs.

Paul, 34, made the first batch in 2007 after being challenged by Fleet Street's star food-writer, Lydia Slater, that he couldn't make the combination work. Lydia dared him to put Marmite into the mix during an interview she was doing for the *Sunday Times*. 'Paul was telling me that there was probably nothing that wouldn't go well with chocolate,' she told me. 'So I said, "how about Marmite?". He didn't hesitate. "I bet I could make it work" he said.' Only a couple of weeks later, Marmite Truffles went on sale.

So how did they go down with Lydia? 'I do love Marmite,' she said, 'but for me, Marmite with something sweet doesn't work.'

But it does for many others. Paul's spokeswoman Kate Johns told me: 'Lydia had the idea, Paul made it work. Now the Marmite chocolates have proved so popular that he'd have a lot of complaints on his hands if he stopped making them!'

Paul, from Trimdon Station, County Durham, who was head pastry chef for Marco Pierre White and is a regular on TV food shows, has two chocolate boutiques in London. One is at 33 Camden Passage, Islington, the other at 20 Royal Exchange, Threadneedle Street, in the City of London. And while each shop is a joy to experience, very shortly it may be possible to get your hands on some Marmite truffles, without going to London. Paul promises that on-line ordering is on its way.

Z

Zambia: A favourite place for ex-pats in the States to get their supplies is from *The Marmite Pantry* website. It exists because the American family behind it have a big connection with the former British colony. Engineer Scott Ferguson, who launched the site in 2005, spent much of his childhood there (Northern Rhodesia, as it was in those days). His parents were missionaries and the family cultivated a taste for what was standard fare for many of their ex-pat British friends. And Scott, who got it regularly for breakfast at his boarding school in the Northwest Province, has never lost his love for it.

On the family's return to the States, there was always a massive problem of finding and obtaining Marmite easily, particularly as they settled in Atascadero, California – halfway between Los Angeles and San Francisco. Out of that frustration *www.marmitepantry.com* was born. At first only Marmite was sold. After five months they started adding a few other British products that ex-pats long for, including PG Tips and Yorkshire Tea. They've purposely kept their range tiny and today have only 11 items, which include - say this quietly - **Vegemite**. And they have a non-food item that emphasises how Staffordshire goods have a special place in the heart of

Brits. They sell 'Brown Betty' tea pots, that are made from the red clay of Stoke-on-Trent, only 24 miles from the Marmite factory in Burton-on-Tent.

Scott's nine children, fifth generation Americans, have inherited his lust for Marmite. The youngest one, 11-year-old Melissa, calls it 'More-mite'. Scott laughed: 'We don't know whether it's a pronunciation problem or just her view about Marmite.'

Zazzle: is a good website for Marmite fans. Primarily it's a place to go to turn your photographs into postcards, greeting cards, posters, or put on all manner of merchandise. But it also has some good Marmite offerings - coffee mugs, cotton shopping bags and t-shirts, emblazoned with some of the best known vintage Marmite advertisements. It also offers a spoof Marmite t-shirt, in Marmite colours with a very definite Marmite logo-look. However the kick comes in the words, which read: Marketing, Generic British Nostalgia, Yesterday's Rubbish Today. It's the fun work of illustrator/artist Dennis Booth. Dennis, from Hyde, Cheshire is, as you might imagine, a definite Marmite-hater. 'I find it really overpowering and too much for me to handle,' he says. *Zazzle* also features a somewhat grotesque, distorted picture of a poor chap with a bugling head. For some obscure reason he's called Captain Marmite. Go to: *www.zazzle.co.uk*.

Zen: for those seeking the path of enlightenment via Buddhism, Marmite could be the food that allows a high level of productive meditation! The remote Samye Ling Monastery in Dumfriesshire hosts retreats for monks who are prepared to divorce themselves from the outside world for four years. Apart from being allowed to receive letters once a month, there is no contact with anyone or anything – bar the dozen or so other monks on the long, long, absence from life outside the monastery walls. There is no television, radio, internet or telephone.

In June 2009 Gelong Thubeten, an Oxford University educated actor who became a monk at 21, left the isolated life of long years of prayer and meditation. On his entry back into 'life', which took him off to Brussels to teach, he talked to *The Times* about his four years of solitude. He revealed that the extreme vegetarian diet would, now and then, be lifted by 'a treat such as Marmite'.

Which is a fitting ending to this A-Z. As it shows that you can get through life without a lot of what a lot of us have! But just a bit of Marmite now and then makes all the difference...

Z: Last letter in the alphabet. End of story? Not necessarily. If you have a contribution send it to: *MishMashMarmite@aol.com* – it could be included in the second edition.

REX ALDRED (cover) bills himself as a 'craftsman artist'. He's a talented painter, photographer and potter with ideas that, when translated artistically, invariably end up with a distinctively off-the-wall but charming, look. Like his latest venture: three-sided plates and dishes. Suffolk born, he worked - while raising his two daughters as a single parent - as a BT engineer. When they were grown he quit work to walk from Ipswich round the coast of Britain. He got as far as Whitby, fell in love with the historic fishing town - as well as his now wife Mo - and stopped his journey.

DAVE JEFFERY (illustrations) from Hillsborough, Sheffield, was 'guided' away from taking up a place at the city art college to become an apprentice engineer. But he always yearned to work as an artist. A step in that direction was when he joined the graphic design department of an engineering company. Finally, in 1998, he quit his job and, with wife Linda and family, moved to Whitby. Today his paintings have a quality that keep the commissions rolling in and he conducts art-courses for a national holiday company. He also designed Deff Leppard's first record cover.

Lightning Source UK Ltd.
Milton Keynes UK
19 November 2009

146469UK00001B/31/P